The Bartender

The Bartender

A Fable about a Journey

MICHAEL MCNICHOLS

RESOURCE *Publications* • Eugene, Oregon

THE BARTENDER
A Fable about a Journey

Copyright © 2008 Michael McNichols. All rights reserved. Except for brief quotations in critical publications or reviews, no part of this book may be reproduced in any manner without prior written permission from the publisher. Write: Permissions, Wipf and Stock Publishers, 199 W. 8th Ave., Suite 3, Eugene, OR 97401.

Wipf & Stock
A Division of Wipf and Stock Publishers
199 W. 8th Ave., Suite 3
Eugene, OR 97401

ISBN 13: 978-1-55635-827-2

Manufactured in the U.S.A.

All scripture references, unless otherwise noted, are from the New Revised Standard Version.

Dedicated to all those who thirst to proclaim
and demonstrate the reality of the Kingdom of God;
and to all those who thirst to receive it.

Prologue

*Do nothing without deliberation,
but when you have acted, do not regret it.*

Sirach 32:19

It is an awful thing to regret one's own life. A person need not be old to carry such regrets. All that is needed is the awareness of the accumulation of wrong turns and poor choices accompanied by the shuddering realization that hope has been lost.

People who lack religious affinities can embrace regret once they recognize that something is horribly wrong with the world and there is no solution to be found. These people might become open to a new search for meaning in life or they might look for the desperate courage to extinguish their own lives in order to eliminate the pain of hopelessness.

Religious people can also embrace regret. Those identifying themselves as Christians—followers of Jesus—are just as vulnerable to the pain of regret as are other human beings. It would seem that Christians might be the brokers of hope, since they seem to hope for heaven after death, hope for a better life before death, and hope that the lives of other people might find meaning and peace with God.

Yet, Christian people still embrace regret and often lose hope. Their reasons differ from the non-religious types in that they do believe there is a solution to the wrongs of the world and that the solution is to be found in Jesus the Christ. Even while believing that, however, they often fear that the paths they have chosen in life have turned out to be outside of God's true preferences. They sometimes fear that God has always had a perfect plan if only the faithful will remain sufficiently devout to find that plan. They cry, "*Your* will be done!" only to puzzle over what that will might be. God begins to emerge as the astonished and secretive parent, watching the errant child wander (often in good faith!) through life, getting everything wrong. It seems to be only when it is too late that God reveals the irreversible truth that God's will has been missed. The liberating claim, "God is light" now morphs into the dark epitaph, *God is deceptive*.

Those for whom faith and hope in God remain elusive, regrets become grounded in personal failure. The misguided conclusion might then be drawn that God rejects those who fail.

Those who have found their faith coming alive as they have trusted themselves to Jesus might find regrets that are grounded in disillusionment. They would not cry, "God is dead!" but, rather, *Jesus, what the Bible says about you just doesn't work*.

This is a story about regrets.

1

*I saw all the deeds that are done under the sun;
and see, all is vanity and a chasing after wind.*

Ecclesiastes 1:14

IN THE MIND OF Paul Philips it seemed like a noble act to start up a new church. It was risky, it was bold—and it was probably insane.

Music City Community Church seemed, at first, like an honorable endeavor. As part of a larger association of churches, it shared with those churches values such as authenticity in worship and style, cultural relevance, and openness to all who would come. The church even attempted to relate to the local community by adopting a name that linked it with the long-standing history of music and art development that characterized the city. It was also grounded in a form of Christian evangelical orthodoxy that put Music City (as the church was commonly nicknamed) in a very respectable tradition.

Paul founded and pastored this church, launching out with a desperate hope that this new little faith community would truly make a difference in the lives of people who had given up on God. He'd read a dozen books on church growth and studied the statistics about how often people move from one church to another ("transfer growth" is what they called it). Paul was distressed to learn that most of what passed for church growth was actually this kind of transference. He would frequently hear of a new church that had grown rapidly, giving the impression that the local atheists and agnostics had finally found what they were always looking for. In the end the truth would unfold: The new churches were typically growing at the expense of the other churches in the community. For Paul, this was a form of spiritual misrepresentation. He felt like the church landscape was cluttered with facades that advertised new life only to offer recycled existence.

Paul was not interested in starting up another venue that gave people the opportunity to move from one church building to another. His hope was that this church would be different. He longed for a church that would seek to touch the lives of people disenfranchised from church and, by implication, from God. This church would seek to reach out to those who lived their lives as though God did not exist. This church would proclaim and demonstrate the *good news* of Jesus Christ.

And, ten years later, the church looked almost nothing like what he had imagined.

Even in his disappointment, Paul recognized that this was not a *bad* church. It was made up of people who were committed to being involved not only as members but also as workers and leaders. The people truly seemed to care for one another. He was grateful that they weren't religious phonies or, as his dad used to say, "Bible-thumping crazies." They were real people learning to follow Jesus. He was thankful for that. He was also thankful that they were people who could put up with him. He seemed to hover around the edges of respectability, never quite leaking past the margins of propriety but often willing to move the boundary markers. Paul liked to think it was his visionary wiring that made him this way. His wife claimed it was because he was natural-born agitator.

While Paul appreciated the congregation's faithfulness in corporate worship, he also occasionally stopped to identify the hidden radicals and subversives of his church. He thought of Louise Simmons, a grandmother who worked in the library of a local community college. She was conservative and quiet, yet when one of the student workers was diagnosed with AIDS, she met with him weekly to console and pray with this young man until the day of his death. There was Roger Davis, a middle-aged, recovered alcoholic who volunteered to lead a twelve-step group each week in one of Music City's meeting rooms. And, of course, there were the kids in the high school group who faithfully traveled down to Mexico twice a year to help at the orphanage that the church helped to sponsor. Yes, Music City had plenty of people who sincerely desired to trust their lives to Jesus and to follow him into some fairly challenging places.

But most of the people of the church were Christians the day they showed up at Music City. They had church backgrounds. They had good reasons for coming to this new church but they were, for the most part, seasoned veterans of the faith. There were a small number who had gone through very difficult life circumstances, had given up on God, and then found new life through an invitation to the church. They seemed to hope that they could like God again. That was something to celebrate.

Chapter One

At the same time, Paul was disappointed that there were not significant numbers of people coming to faith in Christ through the ministry of the church. The pastor had hoped to see a church, after ten years, filled with people who would not have called themselves followers of Jesus before they connected with Music City. Instead, those people were a small and diminishing minority. His continuous reminder that this church was called to be "a people for God, for the sake of the world" began to seem like an idealistic dream that could not awaken to some kind of reality.

Paul and other leaders had tried to work through all the blaming and rationalizing that comes with the process of self-examination. They attempted to address the deficiencies that were readily correctable in the church. Some suggested that the vision was flawed in the first place. Others claimed that the chemistry of the congregation was actually quite fine as it was, and maybe it needed to stay that way. Still others hoped that learning to reach out to those on the outside of the church would still somehow happen.

Paul's leadership team consisted of eight people. There were four members who served as the church's board of directors, which was chaired by a straightforward businessman named Frank Osborne, who also devoted a Saturday a month to overseeing the church's outreach to single mothers; Dean Mori, a young man with a sharp mind and a love for learning who served as his associate pastor; and three non-paid volunteers who brought oversight to significant areas of ministry in the church. A woman named Gracie Kline was one of these volunteer leaders and, although she and Paul often butted heads on issues of theology and church life, Paul appreciated her sharp mind and her dedication to the church. While the team experienced inevitable conflicts, most issues were resolved without bloodshed.

One particular exchange, however, that took place on that team over a year ago continued to haunt Paul. It involved a man named Ralph Bennett who had just recently agreed to serve on the board. Paul had asked the team to engage in an open discussion about how the church might reach out to the local community. It was Ralph who responded first.

"Paul, why is it so important to you to bring outsiders into our church?"

Paul could feel his defenses rising up. "Ralph, it's only important to me to the extent that I believe it is important to God. I think the Bible is pretty clear about our mission in the world."

"But I think your first priority as the pastor should be to take care of the people who are already here," said Ralph.

"I agree that caring for the church is important, but that's something we all share in together. The pastor isn't necessarily the only one who does that," said Paul.

"Paul, *you are the pastor*. It is your job to take care of the spiritual needs of the people of your church. This talk about reaching outsiders is fine—if that's really what God wants—but not at the expense of the people."

"So are you saying that I neglect the people of the church?" Paul could feel his face redden.

"Well, let's just say that I think you are in danger of that. Besides—how do you know that God doesn't *want* our church to be small?"

"And why would God want that?"

"Maybe God wants us to find out who we really are. Maybe we need to be in a safe place to do that. What if God doesn't want us to bring in outsiders to mess with the chemistry that we have," argued Ralph.

"I just can't identify with that, Ralph. I believe we are to care for one another, not to be a group that sees the pastor as some kind of parent figure. And I believe we are here to impact our world, and sometimes that will mean changing the chemistry."

Ralph leaned back in his chair and looked steadily at Paul. "I think you should really pray about this, Paul. There might be people who don't agree with what you are saying and could even leave the church."

This exchange was uncomfortable for everyone in the room. Finally a couple of the other team members spoke up, fortunately coming to Paul's aid. Frank Osborne was one who addressed Ralph directly.

"Ralph, I can appreciate your concern about the people within the church receiving pastoral care—something that I hope we are *all* involved in—but I have to say that Paul's interest in outreach is hardly something new. As I recall, it was a fundamental reason for starting this church in the first place."

When Ralph realized that he didn't have the allies he had hoped for, he crossed his arms and remained quiet for the remainder of the meeting. Within the next month he and his family left Music City, taking a handful of people with them. On one level the departure saddened Paul. On another, it was a relief.

The conflict with Ralph brought up a number of Paul's fears. He knew he had strong feelings about certain things, like the purpose and goals of his

Chapter One

church. But he feared the conflicts that seemed to inevitably come with his convictions. Paul's greatest fear was to find himself facing a showdown with the leaders of his church only to find that he had been off-base the entire time. He hated that his self-confidence was so fragile. The confrontation with Ralph was, in retrospect, survivable for Paul because of the support of the rest of his board. Paul's additional fear of finding himself standing alone in his beliefs was, at least for the time being, put back in its dark closet. But he was concerned about the effects of Ralph's departure on Gracie, since Ralph's wife, Sue, was Gracie's close friend.

Paul assumed the church could address its internal organizational issues without a lot of difficulty. Churches did it all the time and it was probably a good thing to go after the obstacles that might have surfaced in the life of the church. He also was aware that the overall culture had changed over the years. It was harder to reach unchurched people than it might have been in years past. The echo of Christian memory was diminishing in American culture even though the language of faith remained alive. This cultural change both alarmed and excited Paul because he was ready for change himself. As much as he loved the church in all its various expressions, he knew that its forms and sometimes distorted messages were not resonating with the people of the western world. There were bigger issues out there that went beyond the friendliness of the greeters or the comprehensive nature of the children's programs. Stem cell research, cloning, and even issues related to American foreign policy were things that Christians were only beginning to come to grips with. The more pervasive sense of distrust in the larger, dominant stories of Christian faith and American destiny were on the block. They no longer held the prevailing consciousness of the culture. Paul often compared this cultural environment to trying to do business during a recession: One might need to use smarter business practices, but would still have to accept the larger reality that the economy was in a recession.

As he considered some of those bigger issues, Paul began feeling like a man who had learned too late not only that he had caught the wrong bus, but that it was also heading off the edge of a cliff.

2

*"Paul, thou art beside thyself;
much learning doth make thee mad."*

Acts 26:2, KJV

Paul Philips often felt like a spiritual misfit. How he ever got into the situation of starting up a new church still puzzled him. His faith in Christ had come alive when he was a young high school student and by the time he started college he was pretty certain that some sort of vocational ministry was to be his path in life. He considered becoming a youth pastor and did some part-time youth work while he went to school. Being a youth pastor had seemed adventurous and exciting. He knew some youth leaders who were almost like celebrities among church groups. Paul thought that wouldn't be a bad way to serve God.

In high school Paul joined a parachurch ministry that reached out to kids in his school. It was fun and he felt like he had an increasing number of comrades in his new faith. The leaders were, for the most part, college students who served part time in this work. They were edgy and cool and the kids really responded to them. He loved how they kept everyone's attention when they had group events, all of which ended with the inevitable call to follow Jesus. Somehow, responding to that call when it came from trendy people made standing up and going forward for prayer a little easier to do. Paul thought he might enjoy being admired by so many kids. He also thought that working with adolescents would fit nicely with his own love of fun.

Over time, however, Paul discarded his celebrity fantasy and finished college. Even though he attended his denomination's Christian university and even majored in Biblical Studies, he knew he wouldn't fit his church's view of what a pastor should be. He asked too many questions and was always trying to fool with traditional conventions of church life. Very often his questioning was rooted in his own youthful arrogance but

Chapter Two

there was also something authentic about his resistance toward religious convention.

When Paul announced to his academic advisor that he was considering a change in his vocational direction the reaction was not what he expected. Dr. Grayson was also Paul's favorite professor and had deeply influenced Paul by his life and teaching. Paul often wondered how a man of such depth and integrity could survive in the denominational fishbowl that had become threatening to Paul. He thought Dr. Grayson would be upset, even reflecting back to him his own sense of somehow letting God down. Instead, he listened to Paul carefully as he described his disconnection from the conventions of church life that he feared would not only cause him turmoil in his professional life but would also consume his soul in the process.

"Dr. Grayson, I keep having this fear that I just don't fit in church life, at least not as a pastor. I watch guys not much older than me who probably were as idealistic as I am right now, and they seem to end up landing out at the margins of religious life and forgetting what was in their hearts. I ran into a guy who graduated two years ago—he was an aide in one of my theology classes—and he's an associate pastor now. Do you know what his big issue was? It was working with the congregation to switch the locations of the piano and organ in the main sanctuary. The church was upset about changing what had always been and he was actually taking the debate seriously! I just don't think I'm cut out for that kind of work. They'd just end up firing me."

Dr. Grayson smiled. "Well, Paul, it's true that church issues can sometimes get stuck on conventional behaviors that are not the essence of the church's life. But do you think it always has to be that way?"

"No, maybe not always," Paul replied. "But there seems to be a lot of it going around. Have you watched these TV preachers? I don't mind the ones that are just televising their church services. It's the ones who grab everyone's attention by claiming to know when Jesus is returning or telling everyone how to vote or just demanding that more money be sent in so that their ministry doesn't collapse. Who cares about any of that? I know I don't. But it seems like too much of church life gets caught up in all that."

"Paul, why are you afraid that what you observe will end up happening to you?"

Paul shook his head. "I don't know. But I just wonder if those other people actually saw these things coming or if the focus on non-essential stuff just sort of snuck up on them. How do I know this kind of thinking won't sneak up on me? I'm afraid I'll start out as a passionate missionary and end up giving out demerits to people who don't come to church dressed the right way." Paul realized he was sitting on the edge of his chair as though he was pleading his case to a judge. He sat back and took a deep breath. "I think maybe I've misunderstood what God really wants for me."

When Paul was finished, Dr. Grayson removed his glasses and stroked his white goatee. "Paul, whether you pursue a life of ministry as a paid vocation or through whatever vocation you choose, you will be continually in the process of learning what God wants for you. Mostly what he wants is *you*. You might or might not survive the demands of the denominational world as a pastor. I think you've got a better chance at success in pastoral ministry than you think. Maybe you've got a kind of unconventional approach to things that is not what you would expect in a traditional pastor . . .

"My girlfriend says the same thing. She told me that I'm probably going to get into trouble because I tend to be an agitator."

Dr. Grayson chuckled. "Well, I might have put it a little more delicately, but your girlfriend may have a point. At the end of it all you will just have to be true to what God has placed in your heart. Once you put your hand to that you will find rest."

"But for now, I'm ready to begin my senior year and I'm wavering about my own direction. Do I just complete my degree and then get a job at a grocery store?" Paul heard his own voice rise as he felt desperation.

Dr. Grayson smiled. "Paul, you've done well in your studies. If I were to base your prospects of survival on your performance in school, then I would say you have an above-average chance at success as a pastor. On the other hand, there's a lot of honest work in the world—including working in a grocery store—and you could just as easily end up there. So, you can take your chances and finish your Biblical Studies degree or change to some other field. Don't let academics box you in the way you think the denomination has boxed you in. There are more possibilities to life than you probably think."

Paul left that meeting wishing that Dr. Grayson had just given him some easy and direct answers, yet knowing that wasn't really possible. He wondered, *How can I be true to what God has placed in my heart when I don't really know what that is?*

That same day Paul decided to talk to his girlfriend, Sheila, about his conflicted feelings. Paul really loved Sheila and looked forward to the day when they could finally get married. They had agreed to put off a formal engagement so that they could focus on their studies. He wondered how she would take the possibility that he might change his vocational direction. He picked her up at her dormitory and drove to their favorite Mexican restaurant. The place was an out-of-the-way, family owned diner that served homemade Mexican food. Paul was nervous as they slid into the booth. As his jeans connected with the vinyl seat, an embarrassing sound barked out. Sheila smiled.

"Better avoid the burrito today, Paul."

"Hey! That was the seat..."

"Don't make it worse by explaining it." Sheila laughed and grabbed a menu.

Over lunch Paul told her what he had been struggling with. He hoped she didn't notice his sweaty palm as he held her hand. When he was finished she fixed him with that look that meant she was about to say something that Paul had better listen to.

"Paul, I know you've been struggling with this for a long time. I'm conflicted too, because I believe God has put some kind of call on your life to lead other people in the life of the church. At the same time, I see how you fight against all the structures and craziness that happens in the church. Maybe it's just that the time isn't right for you. Maybe God's timetable is just different from ours."

Different from ours. Paul wondered if she was referring to a timetable about his life's work or a timetable for their marriage. He suddenly feared that she might be seeing his personal conflict as weakness. Maybe she found that unappealing.

Paul asked, "Will you be disappointed in me if I take a different career path?"

Sheila glared at Paul, giving him that look that both caused him to fear for his life and also made him want to grab her and kiss her passionately. "Listen, buster. I love you because of *you*, not because of your job. Get that straight, OK?" Paul got it.

Within the week Paul made the decision to step away from his Biblical Studies program and work instead toward a degree in history with the hope that he could teach in a high school somewhere. After he graduated he completed a teaching credential and landed a job, as he had hoped, at the high school in Eisington—also known as Music City. After his first year of teaching, he and Sheila were married. Their daughter Lindsay arrived two years later. Tyler showed up eighteen months after that. They had settled into a comfortable, respectable middle-class life. In some ways Paul felt that this kind of life liberated him from the concerns about church and faith that had dogged him in his earlier years.

By the time Paul hit his early thirties, a familiar restlessness began to visit him. While he enjoyed teaching, he had this strange sense that God was drawing him to a riskier place in life. It felt like a call to really trust God and follow what was percolating in his heart. This terrified Paul. He had a young family. He had a good job. This was insane.

After Paul and Sheila were married, they began attending a church that was much less conventional than the church Paul had grown up in during the 70's. The people dressed casually, the music was on the rock 'n roll side, and the sense of God's presence and the call to be a part of God's mission in the world was engaging. It was also part of a church movement that valued the planting of new churches—a concept to which Paul had never given much thought.

Something both wonderful and disturbing happened to Paul during this time. The wonder came as Paul began to recognize God's deep and pervasive love for the world and as he considered the possibility that God was very much at work in human lives. During times of corporate worship with this casual crowd Paul often felt like God was really present as the people sang and raised their hands upward in expectant adoration. He believed that God was *always* present no matter what. These times of worship, however, made that belief tangible and real to him.

What was disturbing to Paul was the growing conviction that following after this ever-present, ever-working God was the most important thing in the world. His old fear of being absorbed into marginal life activities resurfaced. It wasn't that he despised his work or his life with his family; it was that, for him, following Jesus was a call that was demanding more of him than his comfortable life seemed to permit. He realized that

Chapter Two

he would rather be uncomfortable in following Jesus than to remain comfortable at the margins of his faith.

When their children, Lindsay and Tyler, were born, Paul wondered if he would become more cautious in his sense of risky faith. Lindsay was almost two years older than Tyler. She was so bright and athletic—volleyball would become her sport of choice—that Paul never ceased to marvel at her. Tyler was the thoughtful and artistic member of the family. Paul loved Tyler's budding creativity. Paul was concerned that his own zeal in following Jesus might somehow derail the beauty and wonder that he saw in his children.

Nevertheless, after a great deal of agonizing prayer, conversation, consultation, and argumentation, Paul and Sheila lurched toward the conclusion that God was leading them to invest themselves in the planting of a new church on the other side of town. Their own church leadership agreed with this and helped them get started. Paul began attending a local seminary on a part-time basis. There was great hope that Music City Community Church would have a huge impact on the people it wanted to reach.

Ten years later, Paul began revisiting his original assessment: *This is insane.*

3

*It is grace, nothing but grace, that we are allowed
to live in community with Christian brethren.*

Dietrich Bonhoeffer

By most Friday afternoons, Paul was ready for Sunday. His sermon had been prepared and practiced, the players were all in place, and the volunteers were ready. Saturdays were usually taken up with morning meetings with people who were not available during the week. Paul also made some attempt to join Sheila in getting the house in order. There were still lawns to mow, repairs to be made, and clutter to be eliminated. If Lindsay had a volleyball game—which seemed, during her senior year in high school, to be every weekend—then he would try to go. If Tyler needed to practice with his band or go somewhere with his friends from the youth group, then Paul usually volunteered to drive.

On Sunday mornings Paul rose at 5:30, made coffee, and talked through his sermon two or three times. When he arrived at church at 9:00, there was still an hour to go before the service began so he had time to make sure everything was in order.

Paul looked over the rows of chairs in the sanctuary. Their dark blue upholstered seats and backs satisfied the comfort needs of the members while the clips that held the chairs together in a line satisfied the demands of the fire department. He adjusted one of the rows, giving in to his private obsession that required the rows to be straight. Paul thought back to his old home church, constructed with old-fashioned pews that were forever fixed in the 90-year old building. As antiquated as that model of church seemed to him now, he still missed the sound of the creaking wood and the smell of the oil that was used to keep the depth of the wood grain alive. As a young person, those were the aromas and images of faith to him.

Even though Music City lacked any sense of antiquity, its converted warehouse *chic* had its own aura of tradition. Paul recalled the centrality of the pulpit and altar in the church of his youth, with the organ and piano

Chapter Three

placed tastefully to each side. That seemed to speak of the church's value of the spoken word and the sacrament of communion, with the music of worship as the supports to the message of the pastor. In contrast, Music City's stage was littered with musical instruments—three guitars, a drum set, a keyboard, and various percussion instruments—pointing to the central place that corporate worship held in the church. His pulpit, so different from the large, immobile, wooden edifice that his own pastor had used, was a simple music stand that often got lost in the clutter of the stage.

While the leased industrial space that made up the facilities of Music City lacked traditional trappings such as stained glass windows, there was no lack of artistic expression. The walls of the entry and main sanctuary were decorated with various commercial prints and even original works by members of the church. Paul glanced at one of his favorites: *The Return of the Prodigal Son*, by Rembrandt. The sense of acceptance and grace represented in that painting always gripped him. Below that print was a collection of drawings contributed by a group of fourth-graders, offering their own interpretations of that poignant story told by Jesus. Paul reached out to reattach the corner of one drawing that had separated from the wall. The texture of the construction paper felt as sacred to his touch as an ancient stained-glass window.

Paul loved how this simple warehouse facility—a building that could just as easily have been used by an office supply company or a widget manufacturer—had become a kind of sacred space in which people gathered on a regular basis to worship God and share in one another's lives. It spoke to him of the way God transforms the mundane things of the world into the wonders of creation. Even though the building lacked the relics that suggested an ancient faith it still offered a sense of physical holiness that stirred him.

Paul's sense of smell often triggered memories for him. Anytime he and Sheila would wander through an antique store the smell of the wood would remind him of his old church. His morning arrivals at Music City would usually lead him to the dominant fragrance of his new faith tradition: *Coffee*. Freshly ground coffee was almost a religious value for the people of his church. The people enjoyed the coffee and, for them, it also symbolized and even fostered relationship. For Paul, the smell of coffee would always be linked with friendship and personal connection. He wondered if the kids of his church would grow up making the same association. He hoped so.

Paul stepped up to his designated music stand to arrange the notes for his message—a message he spent ten to fifteen hours preparing. He looked out at the empty chairs and thought of the people who would soon fill them and hoped they would enjoy the very sensory experience of it all. Paul closed his eyes and imagined the sounds of people settling in their seats after worshipping in song, the smell of coffee from the cups that found their ways under the seats, and the sight of the people themselves, coming together intentionally as a faith community even when others were out pursuing interests that were probably much more entertaining. The experience never failed to give him an adrenalin rush.

With all of its weaknesses and quirks, Paul loved this church.

4

*If you would be a real seeker after truth,
it is necessary that at least once in your life you doubt,
as far as possible, all things.*

René Descartes

"Why do we keep meeting here? I always feel like I'm on the set of an old *Cheers* rerun."

"It's because there's an important community that comes here—one we ought to be connecting with."

"They don't look much like the people in *our* church."

"That's just the problem."

Paul and Gracie met every week at a pub in the local historic downtown area. The building that housed the pub was formerly a warehouse as were the neighboring structures that lined that particular street. The brick walls and heavy roof beams had been repaired and restored but left exposed, giving the pub a connection with the city's early history. The chairs and tables were all mismatched antiques, sometimes wobbly but always offering space for long lunches and conversations. In the center of the long, rectangular structure was an ornate oak bar that stretched out over 20 feet, with a carved back section that held bottles and taps that reached from floor to ceiling. While the pub was more of a restaurant than just a bar, the drinking area provided the hub from which the rest of the seating area emanated.

The old wood smells and feeling of an earlier era filled Paul with a sense of community and human connection. There was a kind of social charm to the place that drew Paul back week after week.

Gracie Kline was in her mid-thirties and a key leader at Music City Community Church. She had come to faith in Christ while in college and soon joined with a large campus ministry. Over time she saw a number of friends become followers of Jesus through that ministry. After college she became a stockbroker and now worked for a large business consulting firm. Even with her demanding schedule, Gracie was a committed and active member of Music City. Because she was single she seemed to have more flexible time than many other people in the church. Gracie was part of Paul's leadership team and she was typically a great contributor, even though she and Paul often disagreed. Gracie seemed uncomfortable with Paul's frequent willingness to question not only the way the church operated but also the so-called rightness of some theological positions. Yet he appreciated her ability to function in a competitive business environment and her persistent objectivity.

"Why is that a problem?" Gracie made a face that revealed her suspicions about the quality of the menu items.

"Look at the population of our church. We end up looking like one another. Most of us are white, fairly well-educated, and able to make a living in this part of the country—which takes a fair amount of money. Yet our community is much more diverse than we are." Paul had expressed this before. It was not a new complaint.

Gracie looked around the pub—an old brick and wood warehouse that had been reclaimed and transformed as the city attempted some form of redevelopment. "OK, so the people who come here are multi-generational, ethnically mixed, and immersed in a culture that tends to be foreign to us. What are we supposed to do about that? Should we implement some sort of affirmative action program? Or maybe we should impose racial and age quotas on membership?" Gracie was becoming irritated by Paul's frequent revisiting of this subject.

"No, I'm not saying that at all. You're right—it would be artificial to start forcing diversity to happen in a church. And maybe it doesn't have anything to do with age or ethnicity, but with people in general. It's just that we seem very unconcerned about the people outside of us."

"I don't think it's lack of concern that's the issue." Gracie moved her menu aside. "I just think people don't know how to get there from here."

"What do you mean?"

"Look. What does the average Christian in the church think about *evangelism*?"

Paul thought for a moment. "Well, they're probably for it, as long as somebody else does it. My experience is that most people see evangelism as a kind of spiritual specialty."

"Right. But even if they thought it was something they should do, how would they go about doing it? You've spoken a lot at church about the

Chapter Four

change in our culture—from modern to postmodern and all that stuff. If *you* read about these changes as much as you do, and yet *you* don't really know how to proceed, then how do you expect the average member of the church to reach out?" Gracie sat back, victorious in making her point.

As Paul sat thinking about what she had said, Dean Mori entered the pub. A recent college graduate, Dean was ten years younger than Gracie and almost twenty years younger than Paul. He was third-generation Japanese-American. Dean was raised in a conservative evangelical church and his college experiences at the state university had served to not only deepen his faith but also to open him up to the complexities of culture, faith, and church life. He was on Paul's staff and served as the youth pastor and associate to Paul. He was also attending classes at a local theological seminary, which gave him continuous material for controversial conversations.

"Hi guys. Sorry I'm late." Dean sat down and looked at his friends. "Did I miss something important? You look pretty intense."

Gracie filled him in on the discussion, trying to downplay Paul's social commentary and focus more on his question regarding evangelism. Dean looked at Paul. "I'm interested in your answer to Gracie's question. I've been thinking about this quite a bit lately."

Trying to buy a little time in order to frame a possible answer, Paul pressed him. "So what are you thinking about?"

Dean leaned in closer. "Well, I don't mean this to be a criticism, so don't take this personally, OK?" Paul knew this meant it *would* be personal.

Dean continued. "Anyway, you know how you are always saying that our church is supposed to be 'a people for God, for the sake of the world'? Well, I've been thinking that the way we operate as a church doesn't really support that."

"What do you mean?" Paul started to feel slightly queasy, taking this quite personally. He had been thinking the same thoughts; it just sounded threatening to hear someone else verbalize them.

"Don't get me wrong. I think the intent is right on. But how are we really helping people to *be* that kind of community?"

Gracie jumped in. "Right. We do a lot of good things. Our gatherings on Sundays might need some work, but overall they seem to be meaningful experiences for the people. We have small groups that help people connect with each other and, hopefully, with God. But we don't really have a way to help them become the kind of community we claim to be."

Paul broke in. "I have to admit that this is really frustrating for me, but I know you're right. Even though we're a relatively young church, we're just as prone to falling into comfort zones as anyone else. I've always wanted us to be a church that grew with people who came to faith in our midst rather than by transfer growth. Instead, we have a church that struggles to grow at all. The people we have are great, but I don't think I know how to help them—*us*—become who I believe God wants us to be."

"I've got an idea about this," said Dean. "I was reviewing my notes from the Spiritual Formation conference I went to a couple of weeks ago." Dean attended this ecumenical conference as part of a seminary class assignment. "There was so much great stuff there about truly becoming authentic followers of Jesus. And I know we keep trying to help people with that through the Sunday messages and in our small groups."

"Do you think we need to do more than that? Aren't people already pressed for time? Just showing up for church a couple of times a month seems too much for some." Gracie sounded a bit cynical, but still interested in where Dean was going.

"I don't know about *more*, but maybe *different*," said Dean, leaning forward in excitement. "For example, what if our small groups became places of intentional spiritual formation—real, authentic discipleship—rather than being simply places of connection? And what if our primary 'programs' focused on real spiritual formation before anything else—even marriages, child raising or whatever?"

"I'm assuming you mean that we should have more of a focus on teaching people to be authentic Christians—which we usually call *discipleship*. I'm always for that. So finish making your connection." Paul felt a growing sense of anticipation, even though he was slightly annoyed that someone as young as Dean was coming up with these ideas.

"Well, that would help us learn more about being 'a people for God.' But the problem is that spiritual formation can become a very self-focused process. Unless there is some kind of outlet for our formation, then we risk stagnation." Dean was on a roll.

Gracie broke in. "I'm a little confused here. What exactly is spiritual formation? I think I know what discipleship is, but this is a new term for me."

Chapter Four

"Well, in a sense spiritual formation *is* discipleship. It is about intentionally orienting your life around God through prayer, worship, and spiritual disciplines like fasting and solitude so that you continuously open yourself up to God and invite him to *form* your life." Dean caught his breath and smiled a little sheepishly. "At least, that's how I see it. The problem with the term *discipleship* is that it has come to refer to a process of learning. It is used too often to refer to the idea of being a student of Jesus rather than one really involved in the life of Jesus. Discipleship is still a good word as long as we use it right."

"Is some kind of intentional outward service the answer to avoiding the introspection trap?" Paul sensed that something was really happening here.

"Well, I think that's an important part. And some sort of corporate service project would be a great unifying thing for our church. But I think that a renewed look at spiritual formation can help everyone learn to see themselves as part of a larger community that is truly *for the sake of the world*—or, to use the nasty word: *Evangelistic*."

Gracie looked skeptical. "Are you saying, Dean, that everyone has the potential to be evangelistic? Doesn't that fly in the face of the idea that only a small percentage of any congregation is actually spiritually gifted that way?"

"What if that research is grounded in a wrong assumption?" Dean had that I'm-coming-up-with-something-nobody-has-ever-thought-of-before look on his face. "What if it defines evangelism in such a way that only the extroverts or fearless people qualify? What if that assumption—probably coming from all those spiritual gifts inventories that are floating around—is based on defining evangelism as making a presentation, getting agreement, and bringing everything to closure through a prayer of faith all in one encounter? If all that is off base, then there is the possibility that a much broader spectrum of people can be involved in leading others to faith in Jesus."

Paul fumbled for his PDA and started making some notes. "So how would you redefine evangelism?"

Dean looked down. "I don't have a strong handle on that yet. But I think it has to be a much more natural thing than we've made it to be. I think it has to pour out of our lives as we are being formed in the character of Jesus. Since we're all wired a little differently from one another, I guess that means evangelism will look different person to person. I really believe we've got to help people learn how to live in such a way that their entire lives are evangelistic. I know that concepts like 'lifestyle evangelism' and 'servant evangelism' have helped along this path, but sometimes I think they still risk allowing people to remain unconnected to other people while trying to let their lifestyles and service speak for themselves."

Paul looked up. "So evangelism, based on what you're suggesting, is potentially the natural outflow of a life of spiritual formation?"

"I think so. I hope so. And isn't that the kind of spiritual journey we want to invite people on?"

"I think we need to start writing this down," said Gracie. "It's probably going to take awhile. Can we order lunch?"

Paul waved to the waitress, signaling that they were ready to order. She was young, in her early twenties, and usually took care of the section where Paul liked to sit.

"Hi, Angie. I think we're finally ready to earn our keep here."

Angie smiled, and rolled her eyes in mock-exasperation. "Well, it's about time! At this rate you may as well stay for dinner."

"Sorry. It's just that we're racking our brains to solve cosmic issues. We're on a mission from God."

Angie put on a look of feigned interest. "So you guys are the Blues Brothers. Er, and Sister." They all laughed.

Gracie looked up over her menu. "So, Angie—got any solutions for us?"

Angie looked down at her order pad. "Nope. No views on the God thing. So what are you going to have today?"

Suspecting they had just moved into sensitive territory, they ordered their lunches. As Angie finished up and left to place the order, another figure moved to the table.

"Hey, everybody. What's going on today?"

"Hi, Emil. Good to see you." Paul brightened up at Emil's arrival.

Emil was the pub's main bartender. He and Paul had gotten acquainted over the years and even ran into each other on occasion at a local coffee shop. Paul really liked Emil and had even invited him to church. Emil always politely declined.

Chapter Four

"You guys look like you're in an intense conversation today. Lighten up—this is supposed to be a fun place!"

Dean laughed and said, "Yeah. We're here talking about church stuff. No fun allowed!"

"Ah, yes. Church stuff. Now I know why you're intense. It does always seem like a lot of work to me." Emil looked sympathetic.

Paul suddenly had a revelation. "Hey, Emil. You might be able to help us with something. You just might have a point of view that would give us a way to get out of a box we think we're in. Would you be willing to get together to talk with me?"

Emil replied, "Sure. Just don't expect anything really deep from me! How about tomorrow morning at *The Grinder*?" Since that was both Emil's and Paul's favorite coffee shop, it was a natural meeting place. It was also close to the pub and made it easy for Emil to head to work afterward. They agreed to meet at 9:00, giving Emil two hours before he had to be at work.

"I'll be there. Thanks, Emil."

As Emil went back to his post, Gracie looked over at Paul. "Doing a little market research, Paul?" Gracie had obviously put on her consulting hat.

"I just have a feeling that someone like Emil could offer a perspective that we don't have. And there's just something about that guy. He seems to see the world in a different way." Paul looked over to the bar, watching Emil serve his customers another round of beers. He was somewhat surprised that Emil had agreed to meet him so quickly.

5

*"'Look, a glutton and a drunkard, a friend of tax collectors and sinners!'
Yet wisdom is vindicated by her deeds."*

Matthew 11:19

As Emil poured the drinks he wondered once again about his place in the work of tending bar. No longer desiring the alcohol himself, he found it easy to distance himself from the effects it was having on the people he served. He always looked into their eyes as they sat at the bar. The people often acted happy and even relieved to be there, but Emil sensed things behind their eyes that belied their apparent contentment. There was even something in him that suffered in the pain that he knew dominated many of the lives that came to sit before him. Yet he continued to give them what they asked, knowing that a kind of leanness was being poured into their souls.

Angie brushed by Emil as she began getting drinks for a table of four. "Hey, Angie. You were sure in a hurry to get away from Paul's table. Everything OK?"

Angie kept pouring and spoke so softly that Emil had to strain to hear her. "Yeah. They're nice people but the *God questions* they always slip to me sort of bug me. It just hit me wrong today."

"Sounds like something is eating at you."

"No, I'm OK." She arranged the drinks so they would balance on the tray. "I don't know. I've just got some stuff going on. It'll all work out."

"You mean, it will all work out all by itself?"

"Yeah, all by itself. That's the way my life works most of the time." Angie picked up the tray and hurried off. It was evident that, at least for now, the conversation was over.

It had been twelve years since Emil got sober. Before that he had been medicating the pain in his own life so regularly that clarity of thought and vision was a rarity. After a two-day, alcohol-poisoned blackout he got scared. When his sister convinced him to attend his first AA meeting, he

Chapter Five

had little hope for any change in his life. But change did come, and the Anglican priest that led the group had helped Emil to start hoping again.

Having his mind clear in the early days of his recovery brought both relief and fear. He was relieved because he felt more in control of his life. But he was also afraid because this new clarity opened up the arena for him to wrestle with his own demons. And Father Tom had helped him with that. Tom had been a good friend to Emil over these difficult and yet healing years.

Emil often wondered how a priest could use the "higher power" language of AA when there would have to be a bias toward the idea of the more personal God of Christianity. He asked Father Tom about that in the early days of his recovery, but the answer was always, "If there really is a 'higher power,' then ask that power to give you the answer." The priest was being cagey, but Emil suspected that this man would help him to find some answers in his life. Over the years, his suspicions proved to be right.

So now, twelve years later, Emil was clean and sober and making a living by serving up drinks to people who were probably just like him. At times Emil felt like he ought to quit and stop helping people to medicate their painful lives with booze, but something kept him desiring to stay close and connected with these people. He had come to believe that it was this "higher power"—which had indeed become quite personal for him—that compelled him to stay. And Emil daily looked for where this power might be at work in the lives of the suffering people he served.

Emil headed for the door of the pub's office to pick up a fresh order pad. Angie caught him before he went in and stopped him.

"Emil, I'm sorry I was rude to you. I shouldn't have just run off like that."

He smiled at her. "Don't worry about that, Angie. Hey, you're at work! You're supposed to be in a hurry!"

She smiled. "I'm just in a really rough place right now. I'll try not to let it show so much here at work."

The sadness in her eyes captured Emil and that familiar feeling that something important was going on hit him. "Angie, I don't want to intrude on your life so it's OK if you tell me to back off. But I want you to know that I'd really like to hear about what's going on for you. I don't want to tell you how to live your life, but sometimes it just helps to get someone to listen to you. I'm learning to be sort of good at that. I also need you to know that while I like you, I'm not trying to hit on you. I'm at least fifteen years older than you and I don't want to come across like a dirty old man."

Angie laughed and shook her head. "No, you're not the dirty old man type." She looked at the ground and became quiet. "I don't know. Maybe. No, I . . . Well, let me think about it."

"No problem, Angie. You know where to find me."

6

*The church with no great anguish on its heart
has no great music on its lips.*

Karl Barth

"I THINK YOUR FRIEND Emil is hitting on our waitress." Gracie sent a disapproving glance in the direction of the office. Emil seemed to fit the stereotypical lusty male that Gracie found so offensive. The bartender was tan and good-looking, with a blond ponytail that reached down the middle of his back. "You men are so predictable."

Dean looked offended. "Hey. Don't lump us all together, please. Just because a bartender flirts with a girl in the pub—hardly a big surprise—doesn't mean we're all animals. Except for Paul here, of course."

"OK, you two. Very funny," said Paul. "Let's leave the drama for a minute and talk this through some more before our time is up. Dean, go back to what you were saying, about evangelism flowing out of a life of spiritual formation. Why is that any different from what people have been saying for a long time? It's not new information that our lives, as Christians, are supposed to have a quality to them that speaks of what God has done in us and what he can do for others."

"No, that part is nothing new. After all, Jesus says to let our lights shine before the people around us so that they can see our lives and learn to recognize God. But I've just been thinking that so much of what I read and see regarding evangelism is often event- or project-oriented rather than just something natural. I'm probably over-generalizing because I'm only responding to what is visible to me, but I know I really feel the lack in my own life and I think we see it in the life of our church."

Gracie finished up something she was writing in her pocket notebook. "OK, I get the outflow idea. I don't think anyone would argue that point with you, but I also don't see what it changes. Do we just eliminate all the structured attempts at evangelism—no more crusades, no more canvassing, no more 'seeker services'—and just hope everyone starts overflowing with great energy for personal evangelism? So maybe my years in campus ministry were just a waste of time?"

"No, of course not, Gracie. I didn't mean to offend you. I know it would be naïve to suggest something like that." Gracie gave him a conciliatory smile. Dean continued uneasily. "But . . . here's what has been on my mind: Have you guys ever heard of *spiritual direction*?" He leaned forward as he regained his momentum and spoke with an almost conspiratorial tone.

"Sure," Paul answered. "Spiritual direction is something practiced mostly by Roman Catholics, I think. I know it's been around a long time. I seem to remember reading something Thomas Merton wrote about the subject. I don't think you find it much in the Protestant part of the world."

Dean started to get excited. "Yes! In my Spiritual Formation course Merton's *Spiritual Direction and Meditation* is one of our textbooks. He talks about spiritual direction as a kind of joint effort between two Christians, where one talks and one listens. The listener isn't an advice-giver, but instead listens for what God is trying to say in the life of the other person. The direction isn't focused on controlling the person's life. It's about helping someone respond to what God is doing.

"And this isn't really limited to Catholics. There's a great series of books called *The Starbridge Series*, by an ex-lawyer named Susan Howatch. It's a collection of six books that traces the lives of some Anglican priests from the 1930s through the 1980s in England. And spiritual direction is how they get the help they need when they get into trouble."

Gracie looked puzzled. "I don't get what this has to do with evangelism. Spiritual direction sounds like something Christians do for each other. How does someone who isn't a Christian end up in that kind of relationship?"

"Thomas Merton would probably agree with you. He pretty much limited spiritual direction to those who were already Christians." Dean hesitated. "I really like Merton, but I think that his limitation has to be challenged. I think we have to start realizing that God isn't just at work in the lives of Christians. God's at work in everyone, whether they know it or not."

"So God was at work in Hitler?"

Chapter Six

"Gracie, I'm not going to try to figure that one out. But if God really loves the whole world, like Jesus said, then that means something for every person, doesn't it?"

"It's prevenience." Dean and Gracie both looked at Paul.

"It's what?" asked Gracie.

Paul smiled. "*Prevenience.* It's an old theological term that refers to God being at work in the world before any of us show up. It assumes God's prior presence in all things—creation, redemption, salvation, everything. It's funny—I've never thought about applying that to evangelism. I've usually thought about people being a kind of blank slate in terms of God until someone shows up to explain that God exists, Jesus died for them, and so on. The idea of God already being at work is interesting."

"But that's no big deal." Gracie was getting impatient. "In campus ministry we always assumed that the people who responded to us were already being impacted by the Holy Spirit. Isn't that the same thing? I don't think this is anything new."

"But don't we usually think that way in terms of God preparing someone to hear our message? What if it's much bigger than that?" Dean smiled as his own sense of discovery came to the surface. "What if God, who loves the world—even though it's all screwed up—is still working to guide, to comfort, to redirect, to correct, and even to help people respond to the good news of Jesus? What if, instead of looking for people who want to sit still for our pre-recorded message, our role as Christians was to pay attention to the people around us, to look for what God is already doing, and then help people recognize that? What if our role was to cooperate with God instead of expecting God to cooperate with our programs?"

Paul had been writing while Dean spoke. "Dean, I think I'm getting your point. But take me to a practical level. We've got this church of busy, well-meaning people. How does this begin to happen for them? How do they start to take this on? If there is training for becoming evangelistic spiritual directors, or whatever, then haven't we just created another program for evangelism?"

"Paul, how about if we just started re-teaching all of us what it means to be a Christian, to follow Jesus, to go where he goes? What if we started really teaching about spiritual formation, not as some new technique, but rather as how to order our lives so that we love God and love others? Maybe incorporating the art of spiritual direction into discipleship training would just give us a way to practically follow Jesus. Didn't he say that he only did what his heavenly Father was doing? Why wouldn't we want our approach to evangelism to look like that?"

Gracie had a distant look on her face as old images from her university days flashed through her mind. "I remember walking through my campus, wondering about all the students around me, many of whom were unresponsive to our evangelistic attempts. I so often grieved over them, considering them to be *lost* people. If what you are saying has any merit, Dean, then *I* might have been the lost one. I might have lost out on so many opportunities to spend time with people and look for signs of God's presence. Instead of being a message-proclaimer, maybe I could have been more like a detective—learning to really listen to people and then sort of dust for God's fingerprints. I have to really . . ."

Angie approached the table with their orders. "Anything else for you guys? Are you OK with drinks?"

"We're great, Angie. Thanks." Paul made a mental note to leave a good tip.

Gracie watched Angie as she hurried away. "So let's take her as an example. What do you see going on for her? Do you see signs of God being at work?"

Paul followed Gracie's gaze. "That girl's a bit of a puzzle to me, Gracie. But I don't think we could presume to see anything without some kind of open relationship. Angie would have to trust someone enough to be willing to talk about her own life. I think that's the only way a person could do some spiritual direction."

"I think you're right, Paul." Dean swallowed a bite of his hamburger. "The trust would need to be there. This would mean that people like us would have to be intentional about making friends with people outside of just our church. And we would have to do that out of love instead of trying to make everyone a project. I don't think there is any other way."

7

Hope deferred makes the heart sick.

Proverbs 13:12

Angie thought how clearing the same tables you served would have been a drag except for the fact that the tips were so good. Other places had workers to clean up after people, which gave the servers a higher status, like being a large mammal in the food chain. But here the servers did it all. And they kept all the tips.

These days, the tips were the high point of Angie's life. She was only twenty-three and supposed to be looking forward to some kind of great, adult life ahead, but instead she felt like she was standing on the edge of a dock that hung dangerously over an acid-rain lake, which was normal in appearance and yet completely devoid of life. She didn't know whether she was normal or not. She just knew she was missing any significant sign of life.

As she cleared the beer and martini glasses from the table that had hosted the big office group, she found herself thinking about her parents. Her mom committed suicide when Angie was eleven, leaving her heart malnourished for lack of warmth and nurture. Her dad tried to keep some sense of home alive for Angie and her younger sister, but he worked too hard and drank too much to be any kind of safe presence for them. Two years later he dropped the sisters off at their maternal grandparents' home across town, presumably for the afternoon. He never came back.

Grandpa was distant and disengaged. Grandma ran the house and had her rules, which were enforced rigidly on the two young intruders. Grandma had not asked for this assignment, but took it on because it had to be done.

Angie discovered the medicating value of sex in her sophomore year of high school. Being valued by a boy, even for one night, was soothing and comforting, even when the sex was awkward and rough. She usually felt empty afterward, but she always started out empty anyway so it didn't matter. Even an hour of comfort was worth it.

In that same year she learned that alcohol and drugs could medicate the spaces not covered by sex. Partying became the goal of each week. Even though she still maintained average grades in school, she had an increasingly difficult time looking beyond what each weekend would bring to her.

Angie's sister was five years younger. They remained close until her sister hit junior high school and she began to experiment with Angie's brand of lifestyle. Both girls found themselves absorbed in their own worlds and friends, no longer depending on each other as they once did.

When Angie graduated from high school she worked a few jobs and kept partying with her friends. She had run through a couple of intense relationships with guys, but there was nothing serious going on for her. After a year she started waiting tables and began taking the occasional community college course. She earned enough to get her own place with a couple of roommates.

Now it was five years since she'd graduated from high school. College had long since dropped below her horizon. She still drank regularly but had quit using drugs, except for the occasional joint. Angie saw her younger sister once in a while, but they had grown so far apart over the years that the relationship was strained. The guys still came and went and sex was still a kind of narcotic. But any kind of lasting relationship eluded her. Even this last guy, Brian, who seemed like he had possibilities, ended up discarding her at the end. She was hurt, but it wasn't like she didn't expect this kind of thing. She knew she would get over it. And besides, he had only been gone for a month. But she would remember him for a long time.

All Angie knew was that she felt so *sad*. She wasn't angry or disillusioned. She was just overwhelmingly sad. Outside of her few friends she had little support in her life and no real sense that anything good was coming around the corner. And the problem she was now facing didn't change any of that.

An hour before quitting time, Angie approached Emil as he was clearing off a section of the bar that had been vacated.

"Hey, Emil. I guess I do need to just talk a little bit. It probably won't change anything, but, what the hell?"

Chapter Seven

"How about if we go get some coffee after you're off tonight?" asked Emil. "I'm done a little earlier than you, so I'll swing back over around 8:00 and pick you up. Is that OK?"

"I might need something a little stronger than coffee."

"Trust me, Angie. When you're feeling like hell, it's coffee that you need."

8

Why, O LORD, do you stand far off?
Why do you hide yourself in times of trouble?

Psalm 10:1

By the time Angie finished her shift it was almost 8:30. Emil waited outside, hoping to keep from being drawn into the activity of the workplace he had exited just a few hours earlier. He was wondering if maybe Angie had changed her mind when she came through the door of the pub and began looking around for him.

They decided to walk the two blocks over to *The Grinder* to talk. Emil liked the place because the funky tables and chairs were spread out in various nooks throughout the restored Craftsman house that had become this coffee shop. It offered space for being alone and also for quiet conversation. As they walked Angie talked a little nervously about the last few hours of work along with the usual stories of customer antics and complaints about management.

Emil and Angie had worked together for the last three years but never had any kind of serious talk. Angie always liked Emil but he remained a kind of mystery to her. He was an expert at mixing and serving drinks but never had a drink of his own. He seemed to genuinely like the people at the bar but not in that loud and insincere way that seemed common in places like that. Emil had always been kind to Angie and often helped her clear tables when things were slow for him. Of course, he did that for everyone so she didn't feel like it was especially for her. Emil joked and talked shop along with everyone else, but he never got crass like some of the other guys. There was something really different about him. She was both intrigued and apprehensive. But she also felt like he might be someone who could be trusted. On the other hand, everyone else she had trusted had let her down. She would give him a chance, but her hopes were not high.

Chapter Eight

They ordered their coffees and found a table in a far corner of the shop. It was a quiet night in *The Grinder* with only a handful of people in the room. They would have some sense of privacy tonight.

"Emil, I feel kind of weird sitting down with you and talking about my life. I just haven't done that very much and it feels really awkward." Angie was tense and fidgeted in her chair.

"It's OK, Angie. We're just friends talking, that's all. I just want to hear whatever you feel like saying. I'm a pretty good listener and I try not to give boneheaded advice—in fact, I try not to give advice at all, if I can help it. I just know that I've found it really helpful to talk to people when I've been in a tough place. And sometimes you even find a person you can actually trust."

Angie smiled and seemed to relax a bit. "Yeah, the trust thing is big for me. That's one thing I've learned to be suspicious of."

"Yes, trust is often hard to come by. So what's going on for you these days, Angie?"

As she stirred her cappuccino, Angie gathered her thoughts. The problem was that her thoughts gathered like handfuls of snakes, squirming and wiggling and totally out of order. "It's really hard for me to put into words, Emil. I feel sort of dead-ended in my life. I know I'm only twenty-three but in some ways I feel a lot older. When I look at other people it seems like they are looking forward to things in their lives. I don't have anything I'm looking forward to. And it's not like I don't like my job; it's actually a cool place to work and the money's pretty good. But for me it seems like this is as good as it gets." She took a deep breath, like she had just finished her turn in a spelling bee.

Emil waited a second or two, then asked, "What are the kinds of things you might want to look forward to?"

"I don't know. Other people seem to look forward to careers and marriage and family and big vacations and things like that. I guess I just don't know if I'm even able to do any of those things. My own idea of family is pretty screwed up. I don't know if I would ever want to repeat that scenario. And I'm not really prepared for anything in life except waiting tables. All this just makes me feel really irritable and sad at the same time. I keep thinking there should be better things in life but I'm sure not seeing any of them for myself. Right now it all just seems like crap." Angie took a drink, and her hand trembled as she lifted the cup. This disclosure had worked her up.

"Angie, why do you think that there should be better things in this life?"

She gave him a puzzled look. "Well, isn't that how it's supposed to be? Isn't there supposed to be something better than just getting by?"

Emil smiled. "Yes, I think so. But why do *you* think so? What makes one thing better than another thing?"

Angie was quiet for awhile. This question was something she had not considered before. Wanting something better seemed so obvious to her. "I don't know. I guess it's different for each person. I know my upbringing was pretty bad and I've made a lot of mistakes, so maybe I don't know what would be better for me. I just have this feeling inside me that says that if this is the best I can come up with, then this life is kind of a rip off."

"Where do you think a feeling like that comes from?"

"Well, I guess it's just natural, isn't it? I mean, isn't that just how it is for people?"

"It depends on how you look at the world, Angie. It seems to me that what is 'natural' is what most living creatures do—they survive. All the animal stories on TV are fascinating, but they still show creatures that are born, fight to stay alive, reproduce, and then die. And there's no evidence that they aren't OK with that. So why shouldn't *we* just be OK with that?"

"Are you saying that we should just be content with a crap life? If that's true, then this feeling is just some big, horrible joke!" Angie was starting to get upset.

Emil held up a hand in surrender. "I completely agree with you, Angie. I just think it could be helpful to consider why you have this feeling, why it's so disturbing to you, and where it all comes from."

Angie sat back and relaxed a little. "OK, maybe I have this feeling because I just don't like my life the way it is right now. Maybe I've never really liked my life. So maybe I look around and see that some people have better lives and that seems attractive. But I really don't know how to get there from here, and I wonder if that's even possible. That's why it disturbs me." She stared into her coffee cup for a few seconds and then spoke quietly. "As far as where this feeling comes from—I don't know. Maybe it's just how human beings are made. Or I guess it could be God telling me I've really screwed up or something. Except, I don't really know what I believe about God."

"Did you ever go to church when you were a kid?"

Chapter Eight

Angie shook her head. "No, our life was way too crazy for that. My grandma sometimes went to Mass and took my sister and me, but she never talked to me much about what was going on and we didn't show up enough for me to learn anything. The whole thing about God is really out there for me."

"Is that why Paul and his friends rub you the wrong way?"

"Paul . . . Oh, the pastor guy that comes to the pub. Yeah, I guess so. They're just so outside of my world. When they drop those little *God questions* on me it makes me feel like some sort of weird project. They seem nice enough but I'm just uncomfortable around them."

"Do you think they might believe that God has something to do with a better life?"

"I suppose." Angie started shaking her head. "But I just can't imagine what that would be for them—going to church, talking about religious stuff all the time, never having fun. I just don't relate to that."

Emil looked steadily at Angie. "So, are *you* having fun?"

Angie looked down. Emil thought her eyes were starting to glisten a little. "No, I'm not." She became quiet again. Emil didn't speak either. After at least a full minute, Angie spoke.

"Emil, if there really is some God out there, then why would he let my life just go to hell? In some ways I've always been alone in the world—so where was God when my mom killed herself? Where was he when my dad took off? How come God didn't make sure I lived with people who cared about me? I'd like to think that God is really there, but I sure haven't seen any signs of him yet."

Emil took a deep breath. "I'm sorry, Angie. I never knew that about your parents. That must have been really hard for you."

She nodded as she wiped at her eyes. "Yeah, it was. But I'm over it now. I just need to get on with my life."

Emil sensed that she was angry at her own confession and was working to stabilize her defenses. "You sound like you feel very alone in all this. If God is as absent as you say, and if this feeling of wanting more is so frustrating, what will your next step be?"

"I don't know. I guess I'll just have to look for a different job or maybe go back to school . . . I don't know." Angie looped the strap of her purse on her shoulder, apparently bringing the conversation to a close. "Thanks for talking with me, Emil. I really do appreciate it. But I need to get going."

They walked the two blocks back to the pub, found their cars, and drove home.

9

"O Lord, I am ashamed and confused before your face."

1 Esdras 8:74

Paul opened his eyes as the book he was holding fell from his hands. He was a voracious reader but the evenings were not his best times for that. It took only five or ten minutes for him to lose consciousness when he opened a book after dinner. Sometimes it was a curse to be a morning person.

Sheila and the kids had long since gone to bed. As Paul organized his briefcase for the next morning he thought about Emil. When he told Sheila over dinner that he was meeting Emil the next day, she asked if maybe it would be more helpful to make appointments with some of the professors at Dean's seminary. Paul agreed that those people might be helpful in addressing some of his questions, but someone like Emil offered the possibility of hearing from a person who didn't carry some of the preconceived ideas about church, evangelism, and spirituality that might be common to Christian teachers and pastors.

Paul had been pleasantly surprised that Emil had so readily agreed to get together with him. He wondered if maybe this was one of those *God assignments*, where he was supposed to say something impacting that would change Emil's life. Emil was, after all, working in a bar, hitting on waitresses, and living who-knows-what kind of life.

And yet, Paul was drawn to Emil in a way that was hard to explain. He appeared to be someone who had seen too much of the world but had survived the journey. In the few times they had talked together, Paul sensed that Emil was at peace in his life. This was a real paradox for Paul. Emil just didn't fit in a box.

Paul began thinking about what he wanted to ask Emil. *What is your impression of church? What do you think of Christians? Has anyone ever tried to 'witness' to you?* This was starting to sound like a cheesy survey. Maybe he would just tell Emil the straight story—that he and his friends

Chapter Nine

were trying to figure out why efforts at evangelism by Christians didn't seem to have great effect anymore.

What if that's not really true? Paul wondered. *What if this is just my problem? Maybe I'm projecting my lack of success in reaching people onto the whole of western Christendom.* Yet, the researchers of church life seemed to support Paul's concern. Church attendance figures in the United States were supposedly declining, and while many people reported that they shared their faith with someone over the course of a given year, the number of people claiming to have come to faith in Christ was also diminishing. So, yes, Paul did have his own problems, but it appeared the problem was bigger than him.

Paul's mind continued its private conversation: *What is the real problem here? Are we just not telling the story anymore? Or, if we are, has the culture changed so radically that it just doesn't respond to the gospel?* Then a disturbing thought drifted into his mind like a dark whisper: *What if we don't have the story right?*

10

The prophet is a fool, the man of the spirit is mad!

Hosea 9:7

THE SIMPLE ONE-ROOM APARTMENT was dimly lit. A single bed, two wooden captain's chairs, and a small, three-drawer dresser were the only furnishings. Against the wall adjacent to the tiny kitchen area were several piles of books, neatly stacked yet wanting to tilt like a family of Pisa towers.

Emil sat in the center of the room, his body in a lotus position. A large, cylindrical white candle burned in front of him, resting in a ceramic saucer. An open book lay on the floor to his right.

His hands rested on his knees. Emil was very still, breathing slowly, and his eyes were closed.

11

Death shall be their shepherd; straight to the grave they descend.

Psalm 49:14

THE ELEVATOR WAS IN a slow descent. Typical of elevator passengers, she stood facing the door waiting to arrive . . . somewhere. She was vaguely aware of someone standing slightly behind her and to her right. Elevator etiquette required her to keep to herself, eyes forward.

She knew that the building itself was not particularly old, but it was rickety. The elevator was tastefully decorated with wood paneling and brass fittings, but the way it rattled made her think more of an ancient lift in an old warehouse.

Something was not right. The elevator made no sign of stopping. In fact, it seemed to be increasing in speed. She began to get a bit nervous. Surely it would slow down any time now, offering a soft pillow-landing and ringing out that reassuring tone signaling the arrival of the desired floor.

There was no doubt about it: The elevator was gaining speed. How tall could this building be? Why was this thing moving so fast? The elevator lurched and she could hear something above her snap and pound against the open shaft. The elevator began to drop with a maniacal ferocity, lifting her a foot off the floor.

It was free-falling. She knew she was about to die. She was not aware of any sudden panoramas of her life flashing before her eyes from a fuzzy cosmic projector. There was no unexplainable sense of peace. All she felt was terror.

Her screams were muted by the obscene shrieking of the elevator as it ricocheted off the sides of the shaft. She grabbed for the brass rail to her right but collapsed against it, hitting her head on the wall as the elevator pitched again. She was stunned, and crying now as her heart froze in her chest. The last feeling she had, however, was not so much fear as it was desperate loneliness.

The elevator exploded like a box of hand grenades when it hit the cold cement bottom. There had been no safety brake and there was nothing below to soften the impact. She could hear herself screaming with a voice that was born in despair even more than it was in fear.

Angie bolted upright as her roommate shook her awake. As her crying and hyper-ventilation gradually ceased, Angie looked at her friend with her eyes wide in an expression of shock. Her hands were trembling as she reached up to place them on her face.

Her roommate hugged Angie and stroked her hair. "It's OK, Angie. You were only dreaming."

12

"Did not our hearts burn within us . . . ?"

Luke 24:32

Paul arrived at *The Grinder* at 9:00. He figured Emil would be like some of the other single guys he knew—laid back and not too uptight about punctuality. To his surprise, Emil had already arrived. He was seated with a cup of tea in front of him. His face was toward the table as he wrote in a spiral-bound notebook. A closed book was at his elbow.

As Paul approached, Emil looked up, smiled, and gathered his materials and put them on the floor under his chair. "Hey, Paul."

"Hi, Emil. It looks like you're an early starter. What are you working on?"

Emil smiled and shrugged. "Nothing, really. I just like to write down some of my thoughts once in a while. Go get some coffee and come sit down."

Paul headed to the counter and ordered a cup of regular coffee and returned to join Emil. "I really do appreciate you making time to talk with me, Emil."

"No problem at all. I enjoy talking with people. It's sort of what I do."

"Right, because you're talking to people at work all the time."

Emil gave a slight frown. "Well, yeah, there's that, but it's also *just what I do*. Talking with people and listening to them is part of my own adventure, I guess."

Paul wasn't sure how to interpret his comments, but decided not to pursue his own questions about Emil's motivations. "I have to say that I was just a little bit surprised—in a good way—that you would be so willing to meet with me on such short notice. I mean, we sort of know each other but we've never really done this before."

"You know, Paul, sometimes I just get this feeling that something bigger than me is going on. That's when I take certain risks with people.

I sort of get these goose-bump moments that tell me something is worth paying attention to." He chuckled and rubbed his arm. "I'm getting a few goose bumps right now!"

Paul smiled but began thinking twice about what he had gotten himself into. "Well, I hope it ends up being a worthwhile time for both of us, even though you're doing me a favor. Would it help if maybe I tried to sum up what my friends and I have been discussing?"

"Sure, but can I ask you a question first?"

"You bet."

"I know you are a pastor, and I assume you are a Christian. What sort of Christian are you? The Catholic kind, the Presbyterian kind, or what?"

"Right." Paul paused and then took a sip of his coffee. "Well, our church is part of a network of churches that are really non-denominational. But we see ourselves pretty much in the basic Protestant, evangelical part of the mix."

Emil nodded. "Got it. So you're more like Baptists and Methodists than you are Catholics."

"Yeah, sort of." Paul grinned and added, "Plus, we use guitars instead of pipe organs."

"Hmmm. Right. I kind of figured you for a guitar guy."

Paul laughed and glanced down at Emil's cup. He was drinking herbal tea. *Of course. And I should have figured you for an herbal tea guy.*

"Why do you say that, Emil?"

Emil squinted as though he were scrutinizing Paul. "Well, I know that you are a pastor, but I've never seen you in a suit or a collar. You're always pretty casual. So I just imagined that you were more of a guitar-church guy than an organ-church guy."

Paul was intrigued by Emil's accurate observations. "You got me on that one. We try to be more casual in our church because we hope to connect with people that aren't particularly interested in those older styles of church services. Which leads me to why I wanted to meet with you: The leaders in my church and I have been talking about some concerns we have. It's part of our value system to want to share our lives and our faith with people. I've found that, at least in our church, we're not particularly good at that, but that's *our* problem. I'm really wondering how someone like you might view Christianity, church, talking about God, and . . ."

"You mean *evangelism*, right?"

Paul stopped short. "Yes. Evangelism."

Chapter Twelve

"So why do you think your church isn't any good at evangelism?"

Paul hesitated, thinking of how to explain this in a way that Emil would understand. "Well, after ten years we just haven't seen many people come into our church as what we might call 'new converts.' That could suggest that we've been keeping too much to ourselves."

Emil gave a little smirk. "There might be some people who are glad that you keep to yourselves."

Paul rolled his eyes. "Tell me about it. We seem to get enough of a bad image projected on us because of highly publicized church scandals and some of the Christian media. But on that note—how do you feel about that—about Christians telling you about their faith?"

"Well, I really don't have a problem with anybody talking about what's going on inside of them. For me, there's something very real in that. The problem I see is when churches and big religious organizations do that in a way that makes Christianity seem like some kind of big event—like those big crusades. I really don't care that they do those things; it's just that I don't know how that really works to connect people to God. It doesn't have much attraction for me."

"What about when people just talk to you one-on-one? Has that ever happened for you?"

"Sure. I have a cousin who got *born again* and always wanted to tell me about how I could stay clear of hell. She meant well and I really do love her, but she was driving me crazy. I've had that happen only a couple of other times, but in each case I've come away feeling like I was somebody's project. I never felt like a real conversation ever took place. It was clear to me that they had something to say but they didn't seem particularly interested in what was going on in my head."

Paul was feeling pleased. Emil was confirming what Paul had presumed. It was also evidence of what Dean had been talking about: The need to become listeners rather than just talkers when it came to engaging with people about faith.

Emil put his elbows on the table and leaned forward. "Paul, you asked what 'someone like me' thought about Christianity and church and what-have-you. What's 'someone like me'?"

Sitting back in his chair, Paul starting feeling uncomfortable. He thought he had offended Emil. "I'm sorry, Emil. I didn't mean anything negative by that. I just meant . . ."

The Bartender

"That 'someone like me' is someone who isn't a Christian or who doesn't have faith?" Emil smiled slightly. He seemed to be enjoying this.

"No . . . well, what I meant was . . . Look, I know that must have sounded stupid and arrogant. I'm really sorry. I guess I was thinking that you just seem like you live in a world that is very different from what I would expect in a person of faith. I guess I just assumed that about you." Paul's face had reddened and he had suddenly become very thirsty. He took comfort in hiding his face behind his coffee mug, even for a few seconds.

"So, I work in a bar, I probably party a lot, and, since I'm single, I must be either gay or a girl-chaser, right?"

Paul slumped and sighed loudly. "Man. I've really done it. I guess I put you in a box. I always thought I was way too liberated to do that to anyone. Someone shoot me now!"

Emil's laughter gave Paul hope that no offense had been taken. "Let me add another side to the box, Paul. I also practice yoga and do meditation."

Paul's face went slack. "So, are you a Buddhist or something?"

Without answering, Emil reached under his chair and brought up the book Paul had caught a glimpse of earlier. He laid it in front of Paul so he could read the cover:

Holy Bible.

Paul's jaw dropped. "Emil, are you saying that you are *a Christian*?"

Emil relaxed and sat back. "Well, that depends on what you mean. If, by *Christian* you mean a religious right-wing nut, then I would have to say *no*. If you mean someone who claims Christianity as a religion just because they aren't Jewish or Hindu or whatever, then *no*. If you mean *Christian* as being part of the ones who are *in* with God while everyone else is on the *outs*, then *no* to that, too."

"So you're not a Christian?"

"Not if those are my choices."

"Then what exactly *are* you?"

Emil lifted his cup, preparing to drink. "I'm a follower of Jesus."

Chapter Twelve

Paul was dumbfounded. "Emil, that's awesome. I . . . I just didn't know and I feel so weird about seeming to judge you. Please forgive me."

"No problem, Paul. So, maybe we've got more to talk about than you expected?"

"Yes, we do. But I have to ask: Do you go to church somewhere?"

"I do."

"Do you mind telling me where?"

"Not at all. I connect myself to a small Anglican church where an old friend is the rector. He walked with me through my alcohol recovery and I've just continued to be mentored by him, now in this church rather than in my AA meetings. The church is actually Anglo-Catholic, so it's got a lot of liturgy and stuff, which really helps me. It's a pretty small group that gathers there and I'm probably the youngest person by thirty years. But I really love those people. And the whole way we worship together is just so ancient and mysterious. It works for me."

Paul was still a little puzzled. "But what about the yoga?"

Emil now appeared perplexed. "I do it because I have a really bad back. It makes me feel better. Plus, it helps me focus as I pray and listen to God. I even light a candle when I do it—for me it's like the Christ Candle at the center of the Advent wreath at Christmas."

This information began settling into Paul's mind like feathers after a pillow fight. He would just have to sort it all out later. "Wow. I had no idea. So you are more familiar with what I'm talking about than I expected."

"Maybe. So let me ask you something: Why is this *evangelism* thing so important to you?"

Paul thought for a moment. *Emil's in one of those high church environments. Evangelism probably isn't really high on their agenda.* "Well, I guess it's because Jesus directs us to 'make disciples of all nations.' The book of Acts is full of accounts of the missionary efforts of the early Christians and of people coming to faith in Christ. It's just part of our ethic to help people learn to trust their lives to Jesus—to find eternal life."

"To go to heaven when they die?"

"Well, yeah, but . . . that's not exactly what I meant. I'm not trying to reduce the gospel down to a ticket to heaven, even though living eternally with God is an important part of the deal. I mean coming to a knowledge of God's love, of forgiveness of sins through trusting Jesus, and then coming into the life of a church where they can grow and have relationship with others who are on that same journey." Paul felt like his language of *trust* and *journey* set him apart from his more conservative colleagues.

"OK, I get it. And then they learn how to tell other people about what has happened to them."

"Right. And that's part of the issue we've been discussing on my staff. We're coming to the conclusion that evangelism has become an activity that is viewed by many as a kind of spiritual specialty—something done by experts. We're trying to say that it should flow out of a life of spiritual formation—a life of growing in faith."

Emil gave a slight grimace. "So you tack it on somewhere down the road after they pray the prayer?"

"Well, no . . . we don't . . ." Paul felt just a little confused. He thought his thesis was solid. Now Emil was finding a loophole that troubled him.

"I'm sorry, Paul. I didn't mean to get *Gestapo* on you. But it sounds to me like you are critical of evangelism as a broad practice because it seems compartmentalized. Aren't you putting it in another compartment by adding it on to someone's spiritual education like it was a bonus course or something? Doesn't that just make it seem like an 'oh, by the way' method of doing things?"

Paul sat silently for a few seconds. "I get what you're saying. Yes, I guess that is what happens. So you're saying it just becomes optional in people's minds and allows them to get comfortable in the relationships in their church life while seeing evangelism as something that ought to be done but doesn't have to be, or if it does have to be done, then there are experts who are responsible for it. Is that right?"

"I can't say for sure, but it sounds good when you say it." They both laughed. "Paul, here's another question: What *is* evangelism?"

Paul sat up straight. This was an easy one. "It's telling people about the gospel—the 'good news' of Jesus Christ, that Jesus died for their sins, and that by believing in him they can find forgiveness and eternal life." He felt triumphant.

Emil stared blankly at him. "You think so?"

Paul was startled. "Well, yes, I do. Don't you?"

"Paul, the 'good news' is rich and amazing. But I believe that what is at its heart is not the message that Jesus died for our sins."

Chapter Twelve

When Paul was a new Christian, he learned quickly about standing up for the truth of his faith. He had waged a number of debates with people who were either unbelievers or just didn't believe *rightly*. Now he really felt he had grown past that need to be combative and felt he was much more open and tolerant at this stage of his life. But Emil's words caused something angry to rise up in him. It felt like an old dragon waking up from a deep sleep, ready to vomit some fire. He composed himself and then spoke in a calm voice that he hoped would mask his distress.

"Emil, what in the world do you mean? That's right at the center of what Christians believe."

"I know. It just isn't what Jesus said."

"Sure he did. He talked about his impending death quite a bit."

"So, some guy walks up to Jesus right after he goes public and says, 'Hey Jesus. So what is this *good news* I've been hearing about?' Do you think Jesus would say, 'The good news is that I died for your sins'?"

Paul shook his head. "No, of course not. But are you saying the death of Jesus isn't important?"

"No way. Of course it's important. It's how it happened! It really does mean something. But it doesn't mean that 'Jesus died for my sins' is at the heart of the gospel message."

"OK, so what is?"

Emil looked quizzically at Paul. "Hey, you're the pastor, I thought this would be easy for you. Jesus says it right out of the chute. He says, 'The kingdom of heaven is near. Repent and believe the good news.' Sound familiar? As far as I can tell, the message that God's kingdom—the kingdom of heaven—has come is what the 'good news' is all about."

Paul's mind suddenly went back to a seminary lecture he heard about this several years ago. It really challenged and rattled him at the same time, thinking that the gospel was about the kingdom of God. But, after hearing it, he just didn't know how that played out in real life and, over the years, the more familiar message of needing forgiveness for sins just settled itself into his vocabulary.

"You're right, Emil. I get what you're saying. But what does that mean in real life for people? I've always had a hard time making practical sense about that. I've always seen Jesus' kingdom message more about people entering into a kind of faith kingdom after they believed in Jesus."

"A few years ago Father Tom—the rector at my church—talked to me about this and he related the idea of God's kingdom coming to my process of recovery," said Emil. "He offered me a couple of books to read by George Eldon Ladd." Paul nodded, showing his familiarity with Ladd's name. "There were two—one was really big, and one was little. I took the little one. It was called *The Gospel of the Kingdom*. It was pretty heady stuff and there was a lot I didn't really understand at first. But what I did get was that Jesus was saying that God had showed up. God was busy. The things that God wanted for people were the best things in the world and he was about connecting with people *right now*. He wanted to set things right on earth *now*. Sure, the hope of heaven after death was there, but it was a real *now* thing as well."

"How did that idea relate to your recovery?"

"Oh, yeah. Well, before I went to AA I was just trashed all the time. Even when I wasn't completely drunk I felt trashed. If you would have asked me about God back then I would have laughed. As far as I was concerned, there was no evidence for God anywhere in my life.

"But when I started talking to Father Tom when he led our recovery meetings, he started asking me questions that changed the way I thought about God. He asked me what I thought it was that motivated me to get sober. He asked me what was inside me that wanted some kind of better life—or even thought that a better life was possible. Then he started identifying certain *helpers* I'd had along the way—my sister, a friend or two, and then Father Tom himself. He started showing me that God had been busy in my life even when I had no capacity for recognizing him."

"So how does that relate to 'good news'?"

"I remember Ladd saying that the term 'good news' has an ancient Greek military background. 'Good news' happened when a runner came to the generals and let them know that a battle had been won. It was about an army going in to fight for something, then learning that they were victorious.

"So the idea carries through with Jesus. God has invaded earth and has come to rescue people from darkness, from evil, from injustice, and even, in some cases, from sickness and death." Emil added innocently, "Jesus was really into the healing thing as I recall."

Chapter Twelve

Paul wished he had brought his PDA or a notebook or something to take notes on. This was much more than he bargained for. Of course 'the kingdom of God' was at the heart of the message of Jesus—it was the good news. And Emil experienced God's rescuing invasion and victory over darkness as he experienced his recovery. It gave a wonderful metaphor for entering God's kingdom—rescue and freedom from all that seeks to destroy you, and a new life of becoming who God intends you to be. Later Paul would try to flesh out where forgiveness of sins through Jesus' death on the cross fit into the equation. But for now, this was great stuff.

"Emil, this is amazing. There's a lot from my own education coming back to me and I'm seeing a lot I need to revisit. But let me ask this: In your life, has this all resulted in any kind of evangelism that you might do? Are there times when you speak to someone about your faith in order to help them believe?"

"Sure, Paul. All the time, if what you mean is being the runner that offers the news that something amazing has already happened. But I don't think this good news/evangelism thing is just about talking. It's also about being present to people. It's about demonstrating to people that God's kingdom is here and that God is at work."

"How do you do that?"

Emil glanced at his watch. "As I said earlier, I'm a follower of Jesus. I just follow him. And, like he said, he only does what he sees his heavenly Father doing. I try to get involved with what God is already up to. And right now, I've got to get involved with getting to work."

13

In you the orphan finds mercy.

Hosea 14:3

THE LUNCH RUSH AT the pub hit like a rogue wave. Emil felt like he was in a blur for at least two hours as the customers moved in and out, each new visitor claiming still-warm barstools and caressing elbows with both friends and strangers. The traffic didn't slow down until almost 2:30 that afternoon.

An hour later the bar and dining area were back in order. The servers wandered around looking for something to sweep up, hidden glasses to retrieve, or a missed table to clean.

Emil called out to the pub's manager. "Hey, Bobby. I'm gonna take 30 and get a sandwich." Bobby raised a hand in consent, keeping his eyes drilled to the reworking of the shift schedule. Emil left by the back door and jogged around the corner to the Deli where he frequently ate his afternoon meal. Even though he could get free food at the pub, he preferred the break from the work environment. He ordered his avocado, Swiss cheese, and sprout sandwich and a peach Snapple, then found his usual place on the Deli's back patio.

Just as he was taking his first bite, Angie appeared. Emil looked up in surprise, his mouth full of sandwich.

"Hi, Emil. I figured you would be here. I came early so I could talk to you. Is that OK? My shift doesn't start for an hour."

Emil nodded and motioned toward the chair opposite his. Angie sat down. Emil noticed that she seemed both anxious and apprehensive. There was something big on her mind. So he waited.

"I had this dream last night. It was so real and vivid, and it scared me. I even woke up screaming and crying. Both my roommates thought I'd lost it. I don't usually remember my dreams, and even if I do they're always fuzzy and silly. This one was really different. I don't know what it

Chapter Thirteen

means or even if it means anything, but it made me keep thinking about the stuff we talked about last night."

Emil finished swallowing. "I think dreams do mean something once in a while. Do you want to tell me about it?"

Angie nodded. "It was so weird. I was in this elevator in some crummy building. There was somebody else in there, too, but I don't know who it was." She waved her hand in a gesture of dismissal. "All of a sudden the elevator started going faster and faster. Then I heard all this stuff breaking up above and I knew the cable or whatever had broken and now it was falling and I was going to die. I was so scared I couldn't believe it. And then it crashed. It was loud and horrible. Then I woke up. I just never have dreams like that. What do you think it was about? Was it about anything?" Angie sat on the edge of her chair and stared intently at Emil.

Emil remained quiet. He prayed silently. *Father, what is it that you are doing? How do you want me to respond?* He waited a few more seconds, then looked up from the table into Angie's eyes.

"I'm no expert on dreams, Angie. So I can only tell you what comes to mind. Feel free to take it all with a grain of salt." He wiped his hands on the napkin and waited again. The words came slowly.

"The elevator is a fairly small, contained sort of room, isn't it? I think the elevator symbolizes your life—the center of who you are. People usually get into an elevator on purpose and they push the buttons in order to get to the places they want to go. But things started getting out of control and your life—the elevator—started taking on a direction that you didn't expect or want. When the cable broke you knew that there was nothing to stop what was going to happen to you. The crash of the elevator was the natural end to something that was falling and heading for a sudden stop. I think that is a picture of what you are expecting in your own life—a crash."

Angie dropped her eyes to the purse on her lap. She studied the leather strap and worked it in her hands. She appeared to be processing these possibilities.

"You said that you felt scared, which makes sense. Was there something else you felt?"

She looked up. "Yeah, there was. I felt scared and really *alone*. It was like, 'I'm going to die in this stupid elevator and no one is going to help me, no one will care, no one will even know that it happened!' I remember feeling that just before I crashed."

"But you said there was someone else in the elevator with you."

"Yes, but the person was behind me and I never really saw who it was. It was like the person was there but not there. I didn't think it was all that important."

Emil felt something light up in his mind, like a road flare on a foggy road. "Angie, think for just a minute. If the symbols in this dream mean something, then maybe this person means something. Who could it be?"

Angie slowly shook her head back and forth. "I don't know. I just thought it was some random passenger because he—or she, or whatever—never really did anything except *be* there. I never even turned around to see who it was."

"I have an idea for you to think about, Angie."

"OK, so who was it?"

Emil took a deep breath. "I think it was God."

Angie's eyebrows dropped ominously. "God. Why would God be in the elevator with me? And if it was God, why didn't he do something? So, God just lets the elevator—and me—smash to pieces, with him in it? And God gets crashed along with it all? I don't get it."

Emil smiled. "Here's what I think: Your life is moving in a direction that you did not want or expect. Things feel like they're moving faster and faster, maybe even free-falling. You do feel scared, and you feel very much alone. But you aren't alone. God has been present with you the whole time. The problem is that you won't turn around and see him or connect with him. But he stays. He even stays when you are doing things that you think would scare God off. God is prepared to stay with you, even if you crash. It's not that God isn't doing anything or that he's just watching you from some distance. He's experiencing your life with you; he's feeling all your hurts and pain. He's with you, Angie. And I would say that he loves you. He's just waiting for you to turn and get acquainted with him."

Angie had averted her eyes to the empty table to her left. Emil saw that she was starting to cry. After a long silence she turned back to him, allowing the tears to stream down her cheeks.

"Emil, I just don't know what to think. I don't know if you're right or not, but I'm feeling something so weird. I'm still really afraid, but I'm mostly afraid to hope for anything. I always get disappointed when I do that."

"In my own experience, Angie, God isn't disappointing. He's mysterious and usually does what we don't expect him to do. But I believe that God is good and that we can trust him."

Chapter Thirteen

"I just don't know. I have to think about all this." Angie dug in her purse for a tissue. After she dried her face, she looked up at Emil with an expression of resignation. "But I do know that the crash isn't just a symbol. I know it's a real thing."

"Why do you say that?"

Angie stood up to leave. "Because I'm pregnant."

14

"Where were you when I laid the foundation of the earth?"

Job 38:4

THE MEETING WITH THE head of his finance team took a little longer than Paul had planned. He glanced at the wall clock: 3:45. He only had a couple of hours before he would have to race home, have dinner with the family, then shoot back to his office to meet with a study group that he led. He returned a couple of quick phone calls, sat back with a fresh bottle of water, and closed his eyes.

The highpoint of his day was clearly the time he spent with Emil. The conversation was surprising and unpredictable. Emil was not like any Christian—any follower of Jesus—he had ever met. How being a bartender, a recovered alcoholic, an Anglo-Catholic, and a reader of theology all fit together was amazing to Paul. Emil even had this insight into evangelism and the kingdom of God that seemed to come more out of his personal experience than just out of informal research.

Paul felt ashamed that he had made such an early judgment on Emil. Hearing Emil's story of recovery and faith caused Paul to reflect on something he had read years ago about the fallacy of being able to tell who is "in" and who is "out" when it comes to Christian faith. The author had challenged the image of Christianity as a kind of enclosed circle in which it was clear who was in the club of faith. Instead, it described more of an ongoing process of faith, with people at different stages, coming toward God at different paces and in different ways. It would be impossible to make judgments about who is in or out because the process of faith is so complex and varied. It was a reminder that God is at work in all these different people, meeting them in the places they were in—even when those places were outside of religious respectability. Emil was certainly one of those people.

The knock at his office door jarred Paul from his wanderings. Dean stuck his head in. "Hi, Paul. Got a minute?" Paul waved him in.

Chapter Fourteen

Dean was one of several bright spots in Paul's life. They met when Paul spoke in one of Dean's seminary classes on the topic of Family Ministry. Paul had expressed his own interest in learning to become a multi-ethnic church. Dean contacted Paul after the class and they talked about crossing ethnic boundaries in the church. After meeting several times, Paul asked Dean to consider joining the church as his associate pastor. After a couple of months of discussion and interviews, Dean came on board.

Dean was of Japanese heritage. Even though his grandparents were born in California, they were forced into the internment camps during World War II. Dean continued to marvel at their endurance and persistence in their faith. They had long forgiven their captors for that tragic episode in American history.

Because Dean and his parents were also born in the US, their sense of acculturation was built into them. At the same time, Dean was keenly aware of the changing demographics of their community and how often that ethnic diversity was not reflected in the local churches. For him, to come on staff at a predominately white, middle-class church opened up the possibility of seeing diversity come into the life of at least one church in the community.

Paul enjoyed Dean's intellectual curiosity and playfulness. They laughed together but also wrestled with some issues that challenged them both theologically and spiritually. Dean's Christian upbringing had been very conservative, but his experience in the secular university caused him to look beyond his own conservative borders. His choice of a seminary that refused to characterize itself as either conservative or liberal was a step on his expanding journey.

They went over some planning issues that needed to be tied up, and then Paul told Dean about his conversation with Emil. He told the story as it happened, leading dramatically up to Emil's revelation of his own faith in Christ. He decided to leave out Emil's rather controversial observation about the kingdom of God being at the heart of the gospel message. Paul needed some more time to process that idea.

"Wow, Paul. I had no idea about Emil. I can't believe that he's a Christian and has actually read something theological." Dean looked like he was having an epiphany. "You know, Emil does what we've been talking about, do you realize that?"

Paul's face lit up. "Yes, I think I'm starting to get that."

"Paul, think about it: Emil says he goes around looking for what God is already doing. That's the *prevenience of God* idea that you were talking about—something, by the way, that I've been researching today. Emil really believes that God is up to something everywhere he goes—even at the bar!"

"Yeah, and it all seems to overflow out of this life of his where he has actually experienced that for himself. At first I was really puzzled by his talk about using yoga in his prayer time, but then I saw that he just wasn't put off by those kinds of categories. For him it was part of the vehicle of his own spiritual formation. And then he goes to this little church that looks nothing like what you would think an evangelistic church would look like. But his soul is fed there, he has loving relationships, he worships . . . and out of that he follows Jesus into the world." Paul shook his head in an expression of wonder.

Dean sat in the chair across from Paul's desk. "Paul, I did a little online research on the word *prevenience*. I learned that for the Reformers like John Calvin—really, stretching all the way back to Augustine—the idea of prevenience had to do with the conviction that people have absolutely nothing good in them that would allow them to do anything honorable or to even recognize God. It's the idea that all people, by nature, are totally depraved. They can only respond to God and act in good ways when God grants them the grace to do that. And, I assume that means that not everyone gets that grace."

"Right. That's part of a theology that I've always struggled with. Too often the conclusion is that some people are created for heaven and some for hell. But the doctrine of prevenient grace does say that the only way people make a step toward God is when God gives them the grace to do it."

"Yeah, but get this, Paul." Dean pulled a sheet of paper from a small notebook he was holding. "John Wesley had an interesting take on this. He said that prevenient grace is something implanted in all people at birth—like a kind of divine spark, preparing them to recognize God. Then I found this—it was a letter he wrote to a lady named 'Miss March.' Here, read it." Dean handed the sheet to Paul.

Paul was surprised that he had never run across this. He knew that Calvin was considered a significant theologian while Wesley was seen as more of a practitioner, but Paul always loved Wesley's melding of theology and practice.

Chapter Fourteen

Paul read the lines on the paper out loud. "The lengthening of your life and the restoring of your health are invaluable blessings. But do you ask how you shall improve them to the glory of the Giver? And are you willing to know? Then I will tell you how. Go and see the poor and sick in their own poor little hovels. Take up your cross, woman! Remember the faith! Jesus went before you, and will go with you. Put off the gentlewoman; you bear a higher character."

Paul looked up at Dean and smiled. "It's really an old idea, isn't it? Wesley saw God's prevenience as going before us in his mission in the world, loving and caring for people, and even calling people like us to join him in that mission."

Dean sat back and scratched his head. "Yeah, I guess it is old. I feel like a kid who's just discovered something he thinks no one has ever seen before, only to find out that everyone but him already knew about it." They both laughed.

"But, did Emil say how he does it, Paul? I mean, he said he did, in a way, share his faith with others. Did he tell you how? Does it have to do with him somehow seeing God at work in people?"

"No, he really didn't get specific, Dean. My sense is that he just wouldn't think in the 'how' terms, as if he had some sort of method. But I remember the way he engaged with me. He asked some questions, he listened a lot, he challenged me. He did a fair amount of talking, but that was after we established some common ground." Paul paused for a moment. "It was like he was being a spiritual director."

"When you describe it that way, it just doesn't seem very complicated, does it, Paul? At the same time, it does really sound like he's looking for where God is already working—in this case, in *you*—and entering into that work as a listener and guide."

"No, it really doesn't seem complicated, but it is really different for us. I'm coming to the conclusion that we've just been side-stepping some things that have been around for a long time. For hundreds of years Christian thinkers like Wesley have been saying that God somehow precedes everything and, while we probably buy into that theologically, we've never really stepped into it as a life experience, especially when it comes to evangelism."

Dean seemed lost in some corner of his own mind. "Paul, there's something else I want to mention. I'm kind of concerned about Gracie."

Paul was surprised by this turn in the conversation. "What do you mean?"

"Well, she seems really irritated by all the things we've been talking about. I think she's having a problem with us suggesting that some of our sacred theological cows need slaughtering."

"But we're not slaughtering any cows. We're just trying to figure out if we're really in the cow business in the first place." Paul felt nervous. He was aware of Gracie's attitude and had hoped it was something that would pass.

"This might be more serious than you think, Paul." Dean pulled a small slip of paper from his shirt pocket. "This was on my desk when I came in this morning."

Paul took the paper in his hand. He recognized Gracie's handwriting.

Dean—
Give me a call next week.
I want to talk about the direction we seem to be taking all of a sudden.
Please—let's make this a confidential thing.
—Gracie

Paul's heart sank. He had hoped that this dialogue would be creative and helpful in reorienting the church. He didn't expect some kind of dissension to result.

"So, are you going to call her?"

Dean looked distressed. "Yeah, I guess I need to. All I know to do is just listen and hope she's OK."

Paul nodded. He would just have to see how this played out. Dean stood up to leave.

"You know, Paul, I really do want to learn—for us to learn—some new things about evangelism, about engaging with people around us and all that. I think it's why we're here. But even more than that—and I know this might sound a little selfish—I want to *experience* this for myself. I want to get into God's *game*. I don't want to go through my life missing what God is doing all the time. I really do want to *feel* God being at work. I hope that Gracie can see that too. I guess I'm becoming a freak."

Paul and Dean nodded at each other with knowing looks, as though they had just decided to join a subversive political action group. Paul said,

Chapter Fourteen

"Yeah, me too. When Emil talked about trying to get involved in what God was doing in the lives of people, he spoke so casually and contentedly. He seemed to just enjoy the unfolding of the process. I've just been so worked up about all this. I want a little of that contentment."

Dean suddenly produced a goofy smile. "Maybe we could become bartenders."

15

*There is a way that seems right to a person,
but its end is the way to death.*

Proverbs 14:12

When Emil returned to work, Angie was already there. She approached him as soon as he walked in the door.

"Hey, Emil. Don't tell anyone what I said, OK? I'm not even going to tell my roommates, so you're the only one who knows."

"I won't, Angie. I promise." Angie had no doubt that he would keep his word. Emil asked, "What will you do now?"

Angie dropped her eyes. "I don't know. I . . . I just can't see how I can keep this baby. It doesn't make any sense. My life is too stuck as it is." She kept shaking her head as if there were marbles in there that would eventually drop into their slots.

"The elevator is moving pretty fast, isn't it, Angie?"

"Yeah, really fast."

Emil smiled gently. "Do you think it has to crash?"

Angie sighed heavily and looked up. "Where else is it going to go, Emil?" She turned and headed for a table where an older couple had just taken seats. For the rest of the day, Emil and Angie worked around each other. They didn't speak again until the next day.

16

But Mary treasured all these words and pondered them in her heart.

Luke 2:19

It was after 11:00 when Angie arrived back at her apartment that night. She was relieved that her two roommates were still out. She really wanted some time alone.

She had only known about her pregnancy for a week. Telling Emil was a risky move on her part but she had felt compelled to let him in on her secret. She didn't even plan to tell Brian.

Angie knew that Brian was the father. While she had had quite a few sexual partners, she was faithful to each one in his turn. She and Brian had been together for six months and there had been a point at which she really started to feel loved. When Brian broke off the relationship just a month ago, Angie was hurt but not surprised. This was just the way life went for her. She had learned to give up on hope.

The option of abortion had not been an ethical issue for Angie. She merely accepted it as something that was done. After all, she had done it once before, just after she graduated from high school. But something different was going on for her now. She began to wonder if having a child could produce the kind of love she had been longing for. Maybe she could offer to this child something that had never been real to her: A love that would be permanent.

Angie wondered how she could really consider such a thing. Aside from the practical realities like having enough money to raise a child, she almost laughed at the idea that she could somehow provide for another human being something that had always been denied to her. She asked herself what it was that made her any different from the rest of the world.

She began to think again about her dream. Emil asked if the elevator really had to crash. He suggested that the other presence in the elevator might be God, staying close to her even when life was ready to end. She thought: *Can that be possible? Would God somehow have been always close to me, even when I was in such pain and loneliness, waiting for me to turn around and see him there?* She didn't know if Emil was right or not, but something in her really wanted this possibility for hope.

Emil's words came back to her: *In my own experience, Angie, God isn't disappointing. He's mysterious and usually does what we don't expect him to do. But I believe that God is good and that we can trust him.*

So, she thought, *maybe life is bad but God is good.* It was too hard make sense out of any of this. *If God was good, then why wasn't life good?* All Angie knew right then was that life, for her, seemed bad. Her mind wandered to what it might be like to take her own life. That would solve everything, in a way. But that kind of final step seemed too frightening to even think about. She could never do that.

She began to ask herself questions she had not considered before: *Why didn't my parents or grandparents ever tell me about God? Did they know about him but were afraid to tell? Did they live in their own crashing elevators, never turning around to see if anyone was there with them?* Angie began to feel as though she had been denied a huge part of life. It was like learning for the first time that there was such a thing as an ocean when you'd always lived in the desert.

As Angie prepared for bed, she told herself that she had to come back to reality. There was no way she would keep this baby and no way she would end her own life—at least not now. So she would get the abortion. That was one problem she could solve.

Weariness of mind and body washed over her as she laid her head on the pillow. Before sleep came, the thought entered her mind: *Before you go, talk again with Emil.* Yes, she would do that. Emil did seem like the one person who cared. But she wouldn't change her mind about the baby. No way.

17

*So it is proof of God's own love for us,
that Christ died for us while we were still sinners.*

Romans 5:8

EMIL WAS SURPRISED THAT Angie called him early the next morning. She wanted to talk again and they agreed to meet at a little park not far from Emil's place at 9:30.

When Angie arrived Emil was already settled on a bench with a cup of tea he bought along the way. He had a cup of coffee for Angie. He noted that she looked tired. Angie thanked him for the coffee and sat down beside him.

Emil waited for Angie to speak. She seemed to be pulling her thoughts together and he gave her space for that. Soon she looked him in the eye and began to say what she had come to say.

"I really appreciate all the time you've spent with me, Emil. I feel really stupid sometimes because in all of our conversations the topic is how messed up my life is. But you've been great and I don't want to keep dumping all my stuff on you."

"Angie, I don't feel like I've been dumped on at all." Emil looked intently at her as he spoke. He wanted her to know how serious he was. "People have helped me through some very hard things in my life. I believe it's important to do that for other people. And I don't feel like our conversations have been an accident."

"No, I don't think they have been either. I don't understand what's going on, but I'm starting to see that there might be a bigger picture than I've been aware of. The dream thing really freaked me out. I've never had a dream like that before and then all the things you said about it made it seem even more real. It's been on my mind a lot. What you said about God being there when I've crashed has really stuck in my mind." Angie looked down and gently shook her coffee cup, stirring the contents that were rapidly cooling. When she lifted her eyes again, she appeared resolute.

"Emil, only you and I know that I'm pregnant. I don't know why, but I just feel like this is something that needs to stay with me—and, I guess, with you. But I'm not planning to keep the baby. I'm going to get an abortion. I hope I never have to do that again, but I'm going to do it now. I feel like it's the one thing I can do to soften the crash a bit. I'm not going to bring a baby into this life I've made. I'm not going to wreck myself some more by having the baby and giving it away, either. I think that would kill me. I don't know how you feel about all this—and maybe you think I'm awful—but I have to do it."

As Angie was speaking, Emil could feel a weight building in his chest. He believed that Angie had made up her mind and would surely follow through with her plan. The weight continued to build even after she finished talking. It wasn't a weight born of moral outrage or anger. It felt like Angie, in her speaking, had passed to him a share of the burden she was carrying. Emil was feeling her desperation, her fear, her loneliness, and even her newly emerging buds of hope. The feeling could not be categorized by politics or morality. It was a sense of *participation*. His mind jumped to the scene in the last hours of Jesus' life: The detached observer, Simon of Cyrene, summoned from the sidelines to carry the cross that was Jesus' to bear. No more the watcher, forever the participant.

"You've made up your mind?"

Angie nodded. "Yes. I don't know what God really thinks about this, or if this means that he's going to jump out of the elevator and let me crash now. But I just don't see any other way. I'm going to do it."

"When?"

"I'm going in next week."

"I'll go with you."

Angie stared at Emil. She struggled to speak. "What did you say?"

"I said I'll go with you."

"I can't ask you to do that."

"You didn't ask me. I volunteered. If you aren't planning to tell anyone else about this, then you need to have someone drive you home afterward. I'll go with you." Emil became as resolute as Angie.

Angie fixed her eyes on the now cold cup of coffee. Tears began to drift down her face. She slowly nodded her head. "OK. Thank you."

They sat quietly for two or three minutes. Then Angie said, "Emil, I don't know what to make of all this. It's like all this time you've been speaking for God. I don't mean that in a weird, channeling way or any-

Chapter Seventeen

thing. I just mean that you've been finding God in all these wrecked places of my life. And you talk about God in ways I've never heard—so much like you really know who he is. It's almost like having you go with me to the clinic is like God going with me. I've heard enough about the abortion thing to figure that God doesn't like it much. But now I feel like God's going with me. I'm really thankful that you're going with me, but it feels really confusing."

Emil nodded in agreement. "I think it is kind of confusing, Angie, and I don't know if I can really explain how I see it. I've come to believe that God always shows up when we least expect him to—like when our lives are wrecked. A long time ago I thought that the Bible was all about religious rules and myths. But I've since learned that one of the main themes of the Bible is that God shows up when people are wrecked. He's like a loving father who lets his kids go into the world and suffer the consequences of the things they do. Then, when they come limping back home, he puts his arms around them and heals their wounds."

Angie used the napkin from her coffee cup to wipe the tears from her face. "I have a lot of wounds that need healing. I can't imagine how God would want to heal a wound that I'm giving to myself."

Emil looked fixedly at Angie before answering. "All I can say, Angie, is that if you go, I'll go with you."

A quietness settled over both of them. The mild yet increasing warmth of the sun, soundtracked by the singing of the birds, offered a space to them that seemed sacred. After a few minutes Emil broke the silence.

"Angie, I'd like to suggest something to help you to clear your mind on what you are doing."

She nodded. "OK."

"This is something that a friend helped me with once." He pulled his notebook from his backpack and opened it. With a pen he divided the page into three columns. Across the top, over each column, he wrote the words *Me*, *Why?*, and *God*. He tore the page out and handed it to Angie. "Tonight when you get home, give this five minutes or so. Under the *Me* column, write one or two things that you want in life. What those things are is up to you, but they should be things more important than a new stereo or a trip to Las Vegas. Think about the things that really matter to you—things your heart really longs for. Then, in the *Why?* column write down why you believe those things have not happened for you. What is it about you or your circumstances or people that have kept you from having the things you want out of life? It doesn't matter if you are right or wrong about those things—it's just about what *you* believe."

"What will this do, Emil?" Angie was puzzled but didn't seem hostile to the proposal.

"Well, it will help you to see how you are viewing your place in the world. By writing these things down you will actually see your own beliefs about your life on paper. I know that, for me, the process of writing things down was the beginning of the process of seeing what I really thought about myself. A lot of it wasn't very pretty. Before you go through this fairly serious medical procedure—one that has a lot of your own life tied into it—having some clearer thoughts about how you see yourself is important. This is big stuff, Angie."

Angie stared at the paper in her hands. Her response was quiet, yet resigned. "OK. I'll do it. But what about the *God* part?"

Emil took a breath and waited a few seconds before answering. "This is the most important part, Angie. After you've written everything down, stop, close your eyes, and ask God to be with you—and I promise you he will. Keep thinking about that elevator that you're in. God is in it with you. Then ask God to show you what he believes about the things you've come to believe about yourself. Write those things down as well."

Angie looked confused. "Really? I've never done anything like that before. How would I know if what I think is God is just my own mind talking back to me?"

"I thought the same thing when I first did this. But trust me—if you ask God to come, he'll come. Trust that whatever streams into your head is coming from the God you have invited to speak to you. Just try it and see what happens. Maybe you'll find something out about how God heals self-inflicted wounds."

Angie carefully folded the paper and put it inside her purse. "This feels a little weird to me, but I'll do it, Emil. You've been so nice to me—I guess I can do this if you think I need to."

After a few minutes they stood up from the bench, walked through the park, and headed in their own directions to prepare for the day ahead.

18

For the message about the cross is foolishness to those who are perishing, but to us who are being saved it is the power of God.

1 Corinthians 1:18

Conflicting thoughts were at war in Paul's mind. He hoped that continuing the dialogue would help Gracie in whatever disagreements she had. He knew that she and Dean would be meeting soon. Maybe some of the issues could be addressed ahead of time. Paul's conversation with Emil had sparked a number of new thoughts and his own mental processing felt like so many wet socks tumbling in a dryer. He figured that his two colleagues would help bring some direction to all this disruption of the mind.

Paul knew, however, that it would be hard to get the three of them together right now. Gracie informed him that she had some business travel commitments this week that would put her on the road for a few days. Since, however, she would be able to connect with him over the Internet, Paul suggested that they all agree to interact on an on-line discussion board that would not only let them have a conversation free of specific time and place constraints, but would also give them a record of what they discussed.

Paul set up the discussion board and opened the conversation.

Paul	Hi, Guys. I've set up the discussion board so that each new entry will show up as an email so you'll know when someone responds. Thanks for agreeing to this format for the time being. When we last met we talked a lot about rethinking evangelism as the ongoing of process of participating in what God is doing rather than as just an outreach program. Before we wrap this discussion up I would like to talk about some of the how-to steps for something like that. But there's another thing that came out of my meeting with Emil about the basic core of our message in the work of evangelism. So I'm asking you what you think that core message is, then I'll tell you Emil's point of view.
Gracie	This system might be a little impersonal, but I like being included in your conversations even when I'm out of town. I'm in my hotel now. My meetings are done for the day (thank you, God!) and I don't have to be at the next one until 9:00 tomorrow morning. Paul, I'm assuming you are asking what is at the core of the message of the gospel, right? Am I stating the obvious by pointing out that it is the cross of Jesus? It's kind of basic to see the death and resurrection of Jesus as the heart of the gospel. Am I missing something here?
Paul	That's my question, Gracie: Are we missing something here?
Gracie	If we don't center our faith on the cross, then haven't we abandoned Christianity altogether? Is this just an academic question or are you going somewhere new with this? I'm not trying to be cranky here (OK, maybe I am) but please help me with this!
Dean	i thought i would check my emails before hitting the bed. maybe I should just go to bed. ;-) i'm with gracie, paul. I think the cross is central to the message of the gospel. you must have something in mind here.

Chapter Eighteen

Paul	Let me point out something that Emil said to me: If a person were to walk up to Jesus during his public ministry and ask him what this "good news" was that he kept talking about, would he say, "The good news is that I died on the cross for you"?
Dean	maybe not, but he would have said that he was going to do that later.
Gracie	Right, Dean. Everything Jesus did pointed to what was coming at the cross.
Paul	In his opening words in Mark 1 he says "The time is fulfilled, and the kingdom of God has come near; repent, and believe in the good news." It looks like Jesus would say that the coming of God's kingdom is at the core of the good news.
Gracie	So you're saying that the cross isn't important?
Paul	No, I'm saying that the heart of the good news/gospel is the kingdom of God. At least that's just what Jesus says.
Dean	ok, I get what you're saying so far. so link this together, paul.
Gracie	This better be good. I'm really tired and now I'm getting all worked up. I need a good night's sleep.

Paul	Sorry to stir things up so late, guys. Look—just let your minds wander on this a bit. All of us who have been raised up in the protestant/evangelical world have valued Jesus and the sacrifice he made when he died on the cross. That's good and important. But we have also tended to focus on Jesus' death as something that creates a sort of transaction that we can tap into so that we get to go to heaven when we die. I'm starting to see that this has created too small a story. Part of the problem we've been talking about is how evangelism needs to flow out of a life of spiritual formation. But why do I need all that if my spiritual transaction is already completed because Jesus died for my sins? I get to go to heaven now, so just let me get on with my life. But if Jesus was saying that the good news/gospel is about the kingdom of God, then wasn't he saying that God's kingdom is here right now even though it will be brought to fulfillment in the future? If the good news is really about God's kingdom then it's about new life right now, being reformed in God's preferences today. It's much more than just a single transaction.
Gracie	This is too much for my head tonight. I'm going to bed. I'll check in tomorrow morning to see what you two geniuses have come up with. Plus, it drives me crazy that Dean refuses to use capital letters.
Dean	sorry, gracie. i'm a man on the move, and doing that just takes too much time.;-) i'm with you so far, paul. i do recall reading something about jesus inaugurating the kingdom and demonstrating it (healing, casting out demons, etc.) but also that the kingdom was yet to be fulfilled by god sometime in the future. but i still can't help but feel like i'm pushing the cross to the margins of what i believe.

Chapter Eighteen

Paul	I've been thinking about that, because I'm struggling too. The cross was big for the first Christians in a lot of ways, especially since it was recent history for them. In other words, it was big because it happened. Imagine how hard it would have been to try to make theological sense out of the death of a real person, especially for the ones who were there when it happened.
Dean	i guess so. but isn't it limiting to say that god forgiving our sins makes jesus' death just a transaction?
Paul	Yes, it is, and I think that's the point. God's forgiveness of sins is about more than just erasing my slate clean of the bad things I've done. That way of thinking has squared well with western individualism—you know, the "it's all about me" syndrome. Think about the bigger picture of God's salvation. He calls people out (Israel) to be his own beloved people but also to be a blessing to all nations (Jesus mirrors that at the end of Matthew 28). God rescues them from Egypt. After generations of their own unfaithfulness and destruction at the hands of foreign invaders, God promises to forgive their sins, that is, to rescue them from exile. If you look at the larger biblical picture of forgiveness, it's really about God rescuing human beings from destruction and bringing them into the place of his intention. That's what Jesus means when he talks about the kingdom of God being at hand.
Dean	this is really good paul. i haven't heard this stuff from you before. where are you getting all this?
Paul	After my conversation with Emil, I realized he was ahead of me in thinking about the gospel and the kingdom of God. I figured, since I'm a pastor and all, I'd better go do some homework. Hey—it's all there in the Bible. ;-)
Dean	ok. i'm fading out. i'm going to crash and then pick this up tomorrow. thanks for setting this up. Zzzzzzzzz
Paul	Sleep well. See you later.

19

And as well as this, the Spirit too comes to help us in our weakness, for, when we do not know how to pray properly, then the Spirit personally makes our petitions for us in groans that cannot be put into words.

Romans 8:26

For Paul, the weekend was filled with the normal demands of the church. By Friday afternoon he wrapped up his preparation for his message on Sunday and spent the evening at home with Sheila while the kids went to a concert with the youth group. He had a couple of short meetings on Saturday morning, came home and did some household chores, then spent an hour fine-tuning his message.

Sunday morning went well. The attendance was average but people seemed connected to what was going on and appeared to enjoy spending the time together. After the service Paul and Sheila had lunch with some of the newer people of the church.

Later that afternoon Paul found himself sitting alone on his backyard patio while Sheila took a nap. Tyler was over at a friend's house while Lindsay was in her room catching up on homework. He was mulling over the conversations of the last week and then considering the realities of life in his own church.

Paul realized that the *status quo* of his church was not necessarily a negative thing. The people of the church had busy lives that looked like his own. Connection with church—and, presumably, with God—was important but also had to be seen in the context of busyness. That's just how it was. Showing up at church and maybe to a weekly meeting or small group was how people got reoriented toward God. Paul wondered how deep that reorientation really went. Then the thought struck him: *How deep does that reorientation go in me?*

If a church suddenly moved its emphasis from whatever it was doing to guiding people into deep places of spiritual formation, Paul suspected it would be perceived as a change of contract. People would leave. It's not

Chapter Nineteen

that people would be against a deeper, more transformed life of faith. It's just that the change would be disruptive and difficult for some. Yet, Paul knew it was a change he wanted not only for his church but also for himself.

He had read the studies that show pastors to be weak in areas of spiritual health. They tend to pray very little, they don't practice spiritual disciplines, and they take very little time for themselves for refreshment. Paul began to see that the lack of spiritual formation in a church could be a direct reflection of the lack of depth in the lives of the leaders.

Paul had begun to draw up a plan to lead the church into new areas of spiritual formation. He sketched out some classes, a couple of preaching series, several workshops, and even a church-wide retreat. He looked down at the notes he had created. He wondered how he could lead his church in a direction he had never really gone himself. He took the cap off his pen and wrote at the top of the page a word that seemed to bubble up in his mind: *WAIT*.

He turned to a fresh page and began to write up a new plan. It was a plan for himself. He saw that his own life lacked space for significant spiritual practices and refreshment. He spent almost no time in prayerful meditation or contemplation of scripture. He came to the startling conclusion that, while he had been a good student of Jesus, he hadn't been much of a disciple. That needed to change.

Paul stopped in the middle of his writing. *Here I am again,* he thought, *making my plans without any kind of reflection or prayer.* He laid his pen down and closed his eyes.

God, please show me what part of this unrest I feel is from you and what part is just my own organizational restlessness. If there is a change to be made in the life of my church, please make that change in me. I want to live my life in the reality of your kingdom, right now. Please release me from the places where I'm stuck and free me to follow you where you are going.

When Paul opened his eyes he knew his life was about to look different. He still wondered how the changes that were beginning to happen in him would affect the church. He suspected that some people would leave if he began to lead them down a path of deeper connection with God. He remembered that people also left Jesus when he called them to give up their old lives in order to find new life in God's kingdom. Paul understood that he was in good company.

The on-line discussion with Dean and Gracie kept circling through his mind. Paul was concerned that they would somehow start diminishing some key elements of their faith but, at the same time, he knew the conversation about God's kingdom and the death of Jesus was important. He recognized that it wasn't a new topic for theologians and biblical scholars, but it was certainly new for the average Christian. He was especially concerned about Gracie's increasing resistance toward him.

Paul's own study of the Bible had shown him that there were a number of ways the biblical authors viewed the death of Jesus. They used metaphors from several culturally relevant contexts of the day. They spoke of ransom, capturing the image of the slave market, where a person would put himself up for sale in order to settle an unpayable debt. The ransom came when someone paid the stated price, settling the debt but then setting the slave free. There were comparisons made to the Jewish sacrificial system, showing Jesus to be the best and final sacrifice. Pictures of the reconciliation of family members, as in the story of the prodigal son, were held up as illustrations of God's love for wayward people. Yet, it was so common for people to settle into one category that Paul had concluded was not on solid biblical ground: *Appeasement*. Paul was seeing that this category suggested that God was angry about human sin, and the only way his anger could be *appeased* was by an innocent person dying. Or, God's sense of honor and justice had been offended by human sin and he had to be *appeased* by the death of one who was pure in heart in order for the scales to be balanced again. Or, the debits in God's books were so enormous because of human sin that only the death of Jesus could create enough credits to satisfy God. All of these images cast God as a kind of angry, needy deity who depended upon some sort of human transaction in order to find divine contentment. This made the God of Israel more like the gods of the fertility cults or like the volcano god of a 1950's "B" movie.

Paul struggled to reconcile the words "good news" with something as horrible as Jesus' death by crucifixion. He understood that the early Christians seemed to make this link as Jesus himself did. As Paul reflected on this, a favorite passage of scripture came to mind, one that he had typically used to help him appreciate his own sense of vocation:

> So if anyone is in Christ, there is a new creation: everything old has passed away; see, everything has become new! All this is from God, who reconciled us to himself through Christ, and has given us the ministry of reconciliation; that is, in Christ God was recon-

Chapter Nineteen

ciling the world to himself, not counting their trespasses against them, and entrusting the message of reconciliation to us. So we are ambassadors for Christ, since God is making his appeal through us; we entreat you on behalf of Christ, be reconciled to God. For our sake he made him to be sin who knew no sin, so that in him we might become the righteousness of God. (II Cor 5:17-20)

Paul began to sense that the link between the good news of God's kingdom and the death of Jesus was not appeasement of an angry God but rather God's giving of himself, in Jesus, in order to reconcile human beings to himself. It was God's way of bringing people home, so to speak. Jesus said that God's kingdom had come and then he invited people to turn their lives around and receive that good news. Paul knew that the meaning behind the biblical term "good news" had to do with a wartime messenger making the run from the front lines of the battle to the military leaders, letting them know that the battle had been won. *Good news* was, in its original ancient Greek context, about *victory*.

So, Paul asked himself, what was the victory that God's kingdom brought that was somehow culminated in the death of Jesus? He saw that Jesus' own ministry brought life where there was death, healing where there had been sickness and pain, and acceptance where there had been rejection and disenfranchisement. It was easy to see that Jesus' death was the result of fear and jealousy by the religious and political leaders. At the same time, it seems the first Christians saw in that horrible experience something about the intentions of God for the world. Jesus' death—and clearly his subsequent resurrection—revealed God's victory over all the intentions of the world. It showed God's victory over what seemed terminal: Death itself. Jesus' death was a kind of substitution for the death of all the people of Israel—who had been called by God to be God's people and to be a nation that blessed the world—so that a whole new kind of people could be reborn as the ones of God's intention. *In Christ God was reconciling the world to himself, not counting their trespasses against them, and entrusting the message of reconciliation to us.* Paul's heart began to beat faster as he saw that the cross of Jesus was about good news because it was the actualization of all God's intentions: To give all of himself for the sake of the world, that a new people would emerge who would be ambassadors of his good news on planet earth. In a broader sense, Jesus' death absorbed the finality of death for all humans and revealed the possibility that new life could be experienced *right now*. Death and resurrection were not about appeasement; they were about God's love for people—such a great love that he would take all their pain, all their separation, all their brokenness upon himself in Jesus. This was all about good news *right now*, a right now that would be part of God's *forever*.

That's what Gracie had been talking about. Paul recalled the concerns she expressed about helping people to pray a kind of transaction prayer—asking God to clean their slate of sin—and then encouraging them to become disciples of Jesus as though that was a supplement to being forgiven and guaranteed a slot in heaven. Instead, coming to faith in Jesus was to turn and receive the good news of the kingdom of God. It was to turn into a new way of living, a new way of relating to others, and a new life orientation—a life oriented around God rather than around anything else. It was to receive the truth that God had indeed reconciled you to himself in Jesus.

It was this sense of a new kind of life that made Paul even more convinced that spiritual formation was to be at the heart of evangelism. Having a life devoted to God was evidence of having received the good news of God's kingdom. Evangelism was the living out of the vocation of being God's ambassadors of reconciliation.

Paul knew he wanted his church to become that kind of people. More than that, *he* wanted to become that kind of person. Again he prayed:

God, change my heart. Forgive me for wanting others to change and yet excluding myself from the process. Please grant me your power to reorient my life around you. Fill my heart with what is in your heart. Show me what it really means to be an ambassador of reconciliation in the world I inhabit.

Paul had always been suspect of so-called religious experiences. Even John Wesley's famous report of having his heart "strangely warmed" by God's Spirit was something Paul figured happened to others but not to him. When he did experience these momentary flashes of revelation or of a deep sense of God's presence, he knew it wouldn't last and he would inevitably plan to return to the diligence of doing life as well as he could.

Something different was happening to him now. He was feeling something inside. Rather than feeling it in the heart, he felt like he was hit in his abdomen, almost like someone had punched him in the solar plexus. He would later describe it as an extreme sense of grief or emotional pain. As Paul doubled over, tears began to flow freely. He began to see in his mind the faces of all kinds of people—some he knew, others were just faces. As the faces flashed through his mind he felt their own pain and

Chapter Nineteen

alienation—broken hearts, inflicted agonies, sick bodies, addictions, and hopelessness. He was not captured by judgmentalism or criticism toward these people; he was captured by compassion. He truly felt as though he was suffering *with* these people.

As Paul wept he knew he was touching the heart of God. This God had given all of himself in Jesus—who lived, suffered, and died as a human being—and in doing so he entered into the pain and suffering of all human beings. Paul saw ambassadorship in a new way. This was not a vocation of distance or of simply having information that others needed to hear. It was a vocation of entering into the lives of others, sharing their pain, and showing them where the God of reconciliation was already present and at work.

Paul's breath came in gasping sobs and then slowly returned to an almost normal rhythm. He gradually recovered and enjoyed the peace that surrounded him. His heart—his entire body!—did feel strangely warm and also exhausted. But this time he knew there would be no returning to the routines of the status quo. Something new was about to happen for him. He would have to trust the church to God.

20

*"Simon, Simon, Satan has asked to sift you as wheat.
But I have prayed for you, Simon, that your faith may not fail."*

Luke 22:31–32

DEAN ENTERED THE OFFICE building cautiously. His perception of the high-powered business environment that Gracie seemed to be comfortable in made him feel like an alien visiting a distant planet. He was also suspicious of Gracie's insistence that they meet in her business associate's private conference room rather than over coffee at *The Grinder*. Dean figured that Gracie didn't want to be overheard by anyone. This did not look good to him.

The security guard at the lobby desk eyed Dean carefully, apparently noting his out-of-place apparel of jeans, a pullover sweater, and running shoes. Dean asked the guard for directions to the office suite and was pointed to the elevator that would take him to the appropriate floor.

Dean stepped off the elevator, looking first to his right and then to his left down a long hallway. The dark blue carpet and gray-brown wallpaper gave Dean the illusion of floating in deep water surrounded by fog. He padded down the hall and stopped before the designated door. He hesitated, telling himself to remain calm and breathe slowly. He reached out, pushed the door handle, and stepped into the suite.

A receptionist greeted him with a curious smile. "Hi. Can I help you?"

"Yes, I'm here to see Gracie. Gracie Kline."

"Are you here to pick up a delivery?"

"No, we're supposed to be meeting here somewhere."

The young woman removed her headset and stood up. "Hang on a minute." She disappeared down a hallway, then reappeared within a few seconds. "Sorry about that. Follow me."

They walked down a short hallway to a room with a large glass window. Gracie was inside the room, sitting at a long conference table, talking

Chapter Twenty

on her cell phone while manipulating the touch pad on her laptop. She was apparently on the job. Dean was struck with the aura of competence and power that seemed to emanate from Gracie as she worked. This was a side of her he hadn't seen before.

"Here you are." The receptionist ushered Dean into the office. "Would you like some coffee or tea, Mr . . . ?"

"Uh, Dean. I mean Mori. Just Dean." Dean felt out of place and knew he was fumbling his words. "No, thanks. I'm OK." The receptionist smiled as she closed the door and headed back to her post. Gracie looked up and signaled him to an adjacent upholstered armchair. Dean sat down and waited for Gracie to finish her call.

Gracie flipped her phone closed, looked at Dean, and offered a polished smile. "Hi, Dean. Thanks for meeting me here. I've got a packed schedule but I really wanted to speak with you. I figured we would use the time a little better if we weren't sitting in a coffee shop somewhere."

"No problem, Gracie. Since you're so busy, does this mean you won't be meeting Paul and me at the Pub today?"

"Uh, no, I don't think so." Gracie acted uncertain. "I really just want to talk to you and then I'll get with Paul later."

Dean shrugged. "OK. Whatever. So what's going on?"

Gracie closed her laptop and leaned back in her chair, folding her hands in her lap. "Dean, I'm really concerned about the leadership of our church and I was just wondering if you had anything you were struggling with."

"Leadership? What exactly do you mean?" asked Dean. "We're on the leadership team, Gracie. Do you mean us?"

"No, not so much the team . . ."

"You mean Paul, right?"

"Well, yes. I guess I do. Look, Dean. I'm really having a problem with the direction that Paul seems to be leading us. His thing about the cross of Jesus not being the core of the gospel message really bothers me. And the talk about spiritual direction seems really *out there* to me. It feels to me like we're slipping down a slope of mystical liberalism or something. What do you think?"

Dean scratched his head and shifted uncomfortably in his chair. "Gracie, I . . . I think that what Paul is trying to do is to get us to think even more biblically than we were before. I think it's been a healthy bit of questioning that he's been leading us in. I mean, when Paul asked us what the essence of Jesus' message was, the right answer was 'the kingdom of God is at hand.' What I heard Paul doing was trying to help us think about what that really meant—how that was 'good news.'"

Gracie waved her hand dismissively. "Dean, I've been doing ministry longer than you have. I've seen people start drifting theologically and it usually turns out badly. I think Paul's lost his moorings and, as leaders in our church, we need to act responsibly on behalf of the church. And this whole 'spiritual direction' thing..."

"Gracie, if you think back, it was me who first brought up the idea of spiritual direction as a model for evangelism, not Paul."

"Oh. Right. Yes, I guess you did." Gracie gave a brittle smile. "Dean, don't you see how you've been influenced by Paul's wanderings? Look, you're young and still learning. Paul hired you and has brought you into a leadership role. I can understand how you would defend him. But it's time to face some hard issues here."

Dean felt his stomach tighten. A dark little seed began to sprout in his mind. *What if Gracie's right? Have I been led down some weird road by Paul? Maybe my folks were right—that all my seminary training was going to damage my faith. Maybe I'm losing my own foundations.*

"I've been talking some lately," Gracie continued, "with Ralph Bennett, and he reminded me that..."

Dean bolted up in his seat. "Ralph Bennett? You've got to be kidding! That guy hates Paul!" The dark sprout started to recede.

"Oh, come on, Dean. Ralph doesn't hate anyone. He was just really hurt that Paul wouldn't take his concerns seriously."

"Hold everything, Gracie. If you're upset at Paul and now you're talking with Ralph, then this is starting to feel like some kind of mutiny. You really need to talk directly with Paul." Dean was visibly agitated. "Gracie, this whole thing is centered around Paul's desire for evangelism to take place through our church. I thought we shared those desires. Paul has even said that our church needs to look like the community that it lives in, and that having a heart for our community would result in at least some kind of diversity..."

Gracie rolled her eyes. "Oh, right. Paul's own 'affirmative action' plan. So we're going to be a relevant church because of ethnic diversity. Look, Dean, just because you're Asian..." Gracie stopped suddenly as she saw the expression on Dean's face. "I'm sorry, Dean. I didn't mean..."

Chapter Twenty

Dean stood up. "This isn't going anywhere, Gracie. I'm not even going to respond to any more of this. I'm not going to get involved in whatever little conspiracy you're trying to create. You need to stop talking with Ralph and start talking with Paul. You'd better speak with Paul right away about this, or I will. I've got to go."

As Dean opened the door to leave, Gracie called after him. "Just think about what I've said, Dean. If I were you, I'd start facing reality."

Dean stormed down the hallway toward the exit. *If you were me, Gracie, you'd be Asian.*

21

For if any are hearers of the word and not doers, they are like those who look at themselves in a mirror; for they look at themselves and, on going away, immediately forget what they were like.

James 1:23–24

The Tuesday lunches at the pub had been one of Paul's weekly highpoints. He enjoyed meeting with Gracie and Dean but also felt like an in-touch sort of pastor who wasn't afraid to be seen in such places.

But today was very different. As Paul entered the pub and walked toward his favorite table he felt a connection to the people around him that was new for him. There were three or four people already at the bar, apparently drinking their lunches. He was aware of a sudden desire to sidle up next to them and listen to their stories and then offer them some hope for life. He imagined the pain some of them might be living with and felt it settle on his own heart. He glanced around at the various workers in the pub—including Angie—and wanted to invite them all into his home so that he might serve them for a change. Paul smiled to himself as he imagined the scene from the old movie *It's a Wonderful Life*, when Jimmy Stewart returns home after his disturbing vision of a world without him, running through the streets shouting words of love and appreciation to all the people and places he had beforehand taken for granted.

As Paul settled into his chair he saw Emil over at the bar, talking to one of the patrons. Emil looked over briefly at Paul and gave him a nod of welcome, then returned to his conversation. Paul opened his menu while he waited for his friends. As he glanced up over the menu, he saw Dean come through the front door.

As Dean approached the table, Paul knew something was wrong. Dean didn't offer his standard smile, but instead sat down heavily and stared directly at Paul.

"Well, I talked with Gracie this morning. We've got a problem, Paul."

Paul's stomach muscles tightened. "A problem with Gracie?"

Chapter Twenty-one

Dean nodded. "Yep. You've seen how annoyed she's been when we've talked, haven't you? She seemed really irritated at what we were talking about on the online discussion board. I was going to say something after she signed off, but I realized she could read it the next day."

"So what did she say to you?"

"She thinks we're heading down a dangerous road. When you challenged us about what the core message of the gospel is, she decided that you had dumped the value of the cross of Jesus."

Paul stiffened. "But that's not what I said! I said that . . ."

Dean held up his hand. "I know, I know, Paul. She missed the point. But I don't think she *wants* to get the point. It turns out that she's been harboring some stuff for quite some time."

"Against *me*?" Paul suddenly felt like a kid whose friends had just abandoned him.

"Well, yes. She thinks you're going soft on theology. She told me that she sees you leading the church down a destructive path of liberalism. When I tried to show her how that wasn't right, she said you had influenced me too much."

"Do you think that?" Paul heard himself sound defensive.

Dean smiled. "Actually, I was relieved that she didn't think it was *me* influencing *you*." He became serious again. "But Paul, there's something else. You know that guy, Ralph Bennett, who gave you so much trouble awhile back?"

Paul was starting to feel sick. "Yeah. Don't tell me: They've been talking, right?"

"Right."

"Gracie's been friends with Ralph's wife, Sue, for years. I should have known." Paul felt a headache coming on.

"Paul, I'm afraid something bad is about to happen. Gracie sounded like she was about to stage a *coup* or something. Our conversation didn't go well. She made me angry and I even got up and left because I was so mad. I guess it was kind of immature on my part."

"What did she say that made you so mad?"

"Well, she . . . never mind. It wasn't important. She just got under my skin. I told her she needed to talk directly to you. Anyhow, I don't think she'll be showing up here today."

Paul knew that a crisis with a key leader was nothing to ignore. He gathered his phone and PDA from the table and stood up. "I'm going to have to call Gracie right away. She should have come right to me so we could talk..."

Just then Angie approached the table. "Hi. Are you guys ready to order?"

"I'm sorry, Angie," said Paul. "Something just came up. I'm afraid we're going to have to skip lunch today."

As he marched out of the pub, Paul thought briefly about the lines he noticed around Angie's eyes. *That girl needs to quit partying*, he thought, *and get some sleep.*

When Paul arrived back at his office, he decided to check his emails before calling Gracie. He was not only concerned that a key leader would start maneuvering without talking with him, but he was also hurt because he considered Gracie to be a good friend. Paul wished he could have a thicker skin about these kinds of things, but he just didn't. He sat down at his desk and looked at the screen of his laptop. He had several messages, but one stood out. It was from Frank Osborne, who headed his board of directors. Frank was an astute and busy owner of a commercial real estate firm, so unsolicited emails from him were a rarity. He clicked on the message and it opened up. As Paul read, a deep feeling of dread found its way into his abdomen.

> Paul,
>
> Gracie Kline called me today and said she needed to talk right away about some changes in you that she felt were making you unfit for your role as pastor of our church. I stopped her and said we were not going to talk any further without you being present. She seems very concerned and, since she has been a prominent figure in our church, I suggest we meet with her right away. Unless you have something unavoidable, I think we need to meet at your office tonight. Let me know if that works, and I'll call Gracie back.
>
> Frank

Paul sat staring at the screen for several minutes. He couldn't believe this was happening. He would have to cancel his dinner plans with Sheila

Chapter Twenty-one

and the kids, but they would understand. This meeting had to happen, and it had to happen now.

He hit the reply button.

22

> *Truly God is good to the upright,*
> *to those who are pure in heart.*
> *But as for me, my feet had almost stumbled;*
> *my steps had nearly slipped.*
>
> Psalm 73:1–2

"Paul, what kind of meeting *is* this?" Sheila was not taking the change of plans very well.

"Something is wrong with Gracie. She's upset about some conversations we've been having with Dean about evangelism and the gospel and things like that. According to Dean, she thinks I'm off base theologically and possibly a danger to the church." Paul had come home early to talk with Sheila, knowing that his evening would be extended at the office.

"Paul, do you remember all the talks we've had about our family coming before whatever new crisis happens at church? I feel bad about Gracie, but I don't think she should have the right to interfere with your real life!" Sheila was fighting to keep angry tears from arriving.

"I know, I know. I'm sorry. But if I don't deal with this now, something worse will happen. I just know it. I think Frank knows it, too. It's not like him to be so insistent about something this last-minute. You know I try to keep this from happening, Sheila." Paul put his arms around his wife and drew her close to him. Sheila embraced him and buried her head in his shoulder. Paul knew she was crying. After a minute or so she pulled away and looked up at him.

"Weren't we afraid of this happening years ago? This was why you avoided the ministry in the first place. I think you're a great pastor but—let's face it, Paul—your freedom in the way you think sometimes scares people. Sometimes it scares me." She looked for something to wipe her eyes. She located a paper towel on the kitchen sink and dabbed at her face.

Paul was shocked. "Why do I scare you?"

Chapter Twenty-two

Sheila shook her head as she wadded the damp paper towel into a ball. "I don't know. I guess I just don't get so caught up in the theological stuff. I just want to love God and love people and enjoy this life together. When you talk about rethinking things it makes that world feel insecure. I think it probably does that for Gracie, too."

"But loving God and loving people is what I'm talking about, Sheila. I want us to love one another, but that love has got to go outward. And I think getting our minds around what we're about and what we believe is really important. I didn't mean to put anyone in a panic." Paul knew he was raising his voice but he just couldn't seem to help it.

"I know. And I love the part of you that keeps exploring. I guess I'm just seeing that stepping out into some of these places puts us in jeopardy. It makes me wish sometimes that you stayed in teaching and we could just be dumb and happy. Of course, I also know that would never have worked for either of us. I guess I'm just scared for us."

Paul took Sheila's hand and led her to the living room sofa. The kids were upstairs and Paul wanted this time alone with his wife. "Sheila, I'm going to try to do this well. Maybe what Gracie is doing is forcing me to move toward leading our church in a new direction faster than I thought. On the other hand, Frank and the board could end up deciding that she's right and that I'm not fit to be the pastor of the church anymore. I'm not counting on that, but I guess anything could happen."

"And this is supposed to make me feel better?" Sheila managed a half-smile.

"I just want you to know that I won't do anything to jeopardize our family. But if I can't do this anymore, I'll do whatever it takes to make sure we're OK." Paul put on as serious a face as he could muster. "In fact, I'm putting an application in for a low-stress job, just in case. Sheila, I think I really want to become an air-traffic controller."

Sheila became stoic. "Don't push your luck here, buster."

Paul was feeling so anxious about the evening meeting that he decided to shower and change his clothes. Sheila went into the kitchen to put something together for dinner.

Years ago, when Paul first started teaching high school, Sheila almost felt guilty about her sense of relief that Paul did not enter vocational ministry. Anticipating the difficulties of church life for a pastor—and particularly for a pastor's family—made her feel as though they had just dodged a bullet.

As Sheila stared inside the refrigerator, hoping for inspiration, Lindsay walked into the kitchen and stood next to her mother.

"Mom, is everything OK?"

Sheila gulped. "Why, honey?"

Lindsay looked nervous. "Well, I could hear you and Dad talking when I was in my room. I'm sorry, but . . . I even snuck downstairs so I could hear you better. Is Dad in trouble at church?"

Sheila's eyes filled with tears. "No, Lindsay, it's OK . . . I mean, it's just people stuff. It'll work out OK."

"Then why are you crying?" Lindsay sounded scared.

"I don't know. It's just that when this kind of thing happens I worry about our life; and I really worry about you and Tyler."

"Why do you worry about us, Mom?" asked Lindsay.

Sheila was quiet. "I don't want you to get resentful like pastors' kids tend to do. They too often get hurt in the church and then get angry at God . . ."

"Mom, you don't have to worry about us," said Lindsay. "We're not going to get screwed up. You and Dad have been really careful to see to it that we have a real family and a real life. And if we're not screwed up now, then we're probably going to make it OK."

"I know, honey." Sheila reached out and hugged Lindsay tightly. Lindsay spoke over her mom's shoulder. "But tell me honestly. Is Dad in trouble?"

"Well, I don't know if he's in trouble," said Sheila, "but there is trouble brewing. Someone is upset about something and apparently causing a bit of a ruckus."

"Gracie, right?"

"Well, yes, it is Gracie."

"Stupid Gracie. She's always so *right* about everything . . ."

"Come on, Lindsay," said Sheila. "Let's don't start degrading Gracie. We don't even know what's going on yet."

Lindsay sighed and stepped back from her mom's embrace. "I know. I just get mad when people try to go after Dad at church. They wouldn't do that anywhere else." She stuck her hands deep into the pockets of her jeans. "Mom, do you get scared that we might not have a job anymore?"

Chapter Twenty-two

Sheila's eyes started tearing again. "Yes, I guess I do. I worry that, after ten years of being a pastor that Dad would have to start doing some other kind of work that he's not really passionate about. I suppose he could return to teaching, but he's been gone so long..."

Lindsay stared hard at Sheila. "Mom, do think God wanted Dad to start our church and lead it?"

Sheila nodded as she wiped her eyes. "Yes, I really do."

"So what if Dad had to stop leading our church? Does that mean that God doesn't care about any of us anymore? Or does it mean that God wouldn't have something new in mind for Dad—for all of us? It seems to me that God hasn't ever let us down. Why would he let us down now, just because stupid... I mean, just because Gracie is mad about something?"

Sheila laughed. "No, of course God isn't going to let us down. But I really needed to hear that, Lindsay. I think God is speaking through you right now!"

Lindsay smiled at the compliment. "Wow. I never thought about it that way. God speaking through me... hmmmmm. You know, I think God is saying we should let Dad have leftovers and then we'll go out for a pizza."

23

It is not enemies who taunt me—I could bear that; it is not adversaries who deal insolently with me—I could hide from them. But it is you, my equal, my companion, my familiar friend, with whom I kept pleasant company; we walked in the house of God with the throng.

Psalm 55:12–14

Paul arrived at his office at 6:30, a half hour before the meeting with Gracie and Frank was to begin. He sat down in his chair and prayed. *God, forgive me if I've gone somewhere I should not have gone. But I feel that I'm following you in this. I ask for a peaceful and happy end to this meeting tonight.*

At ten minutes to seven, Frank showed up, looking tired like many businessmen at the end of their day. Frank had always been a strong supporter of Paul and had helped guide him in the early days of the church to set up proper business practices. As supportive as he was, he was always firm about doing the right thing. Frank didn't mind challenging Paul when issues came up that impacted the good of the church. Paul had learned a lot from Frank and hoped that when he retired one day—which could be soon, since he just turned 67—he would continue to be free to bring counsel and help to Paul.

Frank settled into one of the upholstered chairs Paul had pulled into his office. Paul had arranged three chairs in a circle so that they could sit across from one another and not be separated by Paul's desk. The two began to exchange small talk about their day when Paul heard the main lobby door open and footsteps coming down the hall. He rose to greet Gracie.

Gracie entered the office looking nervous. Paul could tell by the look on her face that she was wound up but not particularly happy about being there. Paul smiled and was about to say something when he was startled by the presence of another person stepping into the doorway.

It was Ralph Bennett.

Chapter Twenty-three

It had been a year since Paul had seen Ralph. Their parting at Ralph's last board meeting had not been pleasant. When Ralph and his family left the church, Paul had not contacted them. He knew that Ralph had been angry and was probably better off going to church somewhere else. Besides—Paul was relieved to see him go.

Paul was shocked that Gracie would bring Ralph to a meeting, especially unannounced. Paul attempted to put on a hospitable smile. "Well, hello, Ralph. What are you doing here?"

Ralph stiffened, but shook Paul's extended hand. "Hi, Paul, Frank. It's been a while." Paul glanced at Frank. Frank had been present when Ralph had challenged Paul a year ago. Frank looked as astounded as Paul.

Gracie quickly cut in. "Uh, since this was just an informal meeting, I thought it might help to have Ralph here. Sue and I have been friends for a long time and Ralph has helped me to process some of my concerns about our church. I hope it's OK."

Paul was seething inside. Gracie knew better than to pull something like this. This kind of stunt was almost more than he could take.

"Well, Gracie, it would have been helpful to know in advance that someone outside of our church was going to discuss things that are part of our leadership team." Paul wanted to add, *not to mention that Ralph is a jerk*. He hoped to enlist Frank's help. He was sure Frank would insist that Ralph leave.

"It is strange to do this, Gracie." Frank looked thoughtful. "On the other hand, maybe it will help you to express more clearly what's on your mind."

Paul's mind went into overload. *Oh, great, Frank. Why don't we make Ralph an expert advisor for our church, while we're at it?* Paul couldn't believe what he was hearing.

It took everything Paul had in him to not react. He forced a smile and said, "OK. Well, then let's sit down and see what's going on." Paul left the room and returned with a fourth chair for Ralph.

Once they were seated, Gracie took the lead. "Paul, I know that you are probably not happy that I've called this meeting without talking to you first, but I think things have been on a wrong course for some time now. I think you mean well, but I didn't think that our ongoing casual conversations were going to change your direction."

"What direction are you talking about?" asked Paul.

"I didn't know what it was for a long time. All the talk about being more outward focused as a church was great—I've done a lot of outward ministry in my time. But it was the movement toward things like spiritual direction that began to bother me."

"How so?" Paul asked. He looked over at Frank, who remained impassive. He figured that if Frank wanted a definition of spiritual direction, he would ask. He didn't.

Gracie bit her lower lip as she gathered her thoughts. "I know you and Dean have been saying that this all comes from ancient Catholic tradition, but that's not who we are. But I was willing to go along with it, since it really just sounded like Christians counseling each other."

"That's not really right, but go on," said Paul.

Gracie shot a glance at Ralph. "Well, it all sounded kind of *new age* to me, but I figured it would just play itself out over time. What pushed me over the edge was when you started saying that the cross of Jesus was not at the core of our faith."

Paul couldn't believe his ears. "Gracie! You know that's not what I said! I said that what was at the core of the gospel message—the 'good news' that Jesus talked about—was the kingdom of God. I never said that the cross wasn't important."

Ralph turned to Frank and spoke calmly. "You see, Frank, this was why I had to leave. You and the others just haven't seen this gradual movement toward liberalism that Paul has been taking."

Paul knew he should just let Ralph speak, but he couldn't stop himself. "Oh, come on, Ralph. You know that's not why you left. You left because you didn't want our church to have *any* kind of outward focus. You liked things just like they were. You left because you didn't get your way." Paul was letting his anger emerge and that made him even angrier.

"Frank, the whole point is that Paul's theology is not consistent with good, orthodox Christianity. He wants to 'reach out'"—Ralph made quotation marks in the air with his fingers—"because he wants the church to be bigger. Now, I can understand that, at least from Paul's point of view. After all, his paycheck depends on the church remaining a viable operation. But what will people be brought into? A church that thinks that the cross of Jesus is something less than what the church has believed for

Chapter Twenty-three

2,000 years?" Ralph folded his hands and put them in his lap. Paul read arrogance all over him.

Paul felt frantic. This was a caricature of what he had been saying to Gracie in their many talks together. He felt like anything he would say now would sound so overly-defensive that he would look foolish. He didn't know what he could say that would make any sense. Paul was ready to stand up and walk out, when he was hit with a revelation.

"It's interesting that both of you would decide that somehow my exploring of the kingdom of God demeans the death of Jesus. Am I hearing you right?"

Gracie shrugged. "I'm sorry, Paul, but that's what I've been hearing."

Ralph offered his best paternal smile and said, "You know where I stand, and how it has affected my own family."

A feeling of peace washed over Paul. "Why don't we print off the comments made on our online discussion board, Gracie? I think that might help us find out what's really accurate here."

Gracie blanched. She appeared to have forgotten that one of the discussions that she, Paul, and Dean had was now archived on an Internet discussion board. "Uh, what would that do?"

Paul looked directly at her, avoiding Ralph. "It would show what we actually have been talking about. It would also show what I said about the kingdom of God and the cross of Jesus." Paul smiled. "That's what I love about those discussion boards. They give you such a great record." Paul felt like this would stop the accusations and force everyone to see his side. When he was just beginning to see vindication on the horizon, Frank broke in.

"I need to say something here." Frank spoke with an authoritative business voice. The other three gave him their immediate attention. "I'm here as the head of our board of directors. Part of our job on the board is to make sure that some basic governmental things take place so that our church acts responsibly with its resources. We also exist to both support and hold accountable our pastor, and we've trusted him to lead our church in things like worship and ministry and teaching.

"So far, Paul's done a pretty good job. Nothing works perfectly—not in business and certainly not in the world of church. But Paul raised this little group up to become a real church and now, it seems, he might want to take it to some new places and that seems to bother the both of you. There's nothing wrong with being bothered.

"But there is something wrong. First of all, Ralph, you left here a year ago and took some good folks with you. I don't know where they ended up, but I consider that to have been a real tragedy. From what I've seen, you're fine with doing things that destroy the community we have around here. I'm not fine with that, and tonight it's my opinion that counts. I may just be a hard-nosed businessman, but I see what you did as poor form, and it hurt us. And since you've left, you've also forfeited your right to have a voice in our church.

"And Gracie, why you would come to me and not to Paul, and then bring Ralph in here as some kind of consultant, is beyond me. I do love and respect you, but if you were my employee, I'd fire you. But you're not an employee; you're a voluntary leader here to assist Paul. I'll leave your status up to him."

Ralph started to interject something, but Frank stopped him. "As I've said, Ralph, you forfeited your right to have a voice around here a long time ago. I want you both to hear me very clearly: Paul is the pastor of this church. Hell, he's *my* pastor! It's part of his job to help us get on track when we're off and to figure out how God leads us and how the Bible speaks to us. I'll take my job any day over his! So you need to know that I don't put a lot of confidence in what you're telling me. Your lack of protocol only makes me more suspicious of your motives. So this meeting is now over and we can all go home. Ralph, you need to tend to your own affairs. Gracie, you'd better reflect on this and make some decisions. This discussion isn't going anywhere else as far as I'm concerned. Am I making myself clear?"

Paul, Gracie, and Ralph were all stunned. No one had been in a church meeting where someone had been that direct. Ralph was red with anger and Gracie looked shell-shocked. Ralph stood up, glared at Paul, and walked out. Gracie didn't move. She looked up at Frank and started to speak. Paul interrupted her.

"Gracie, there's something more. Regardless of what you think of me—and I have to say again that what you seem to think is not accurate—the lack of protocol in all of this really troubles me. Going directly to the person who has offended you is a pretty consistent biblical ethic, as I recall. But what's really buzzing around in my mind is not that Ralph was involved in this; what's bothering me is that I wonder who else out there is now harboring doubts about me? In other words, who else have you been talking to?"

Chapter Twenty-three

Gracie stiffened at Paul's question. "I . . . there's . . . I've only talked to a few people about my concerns about the leadership of the church, but only to see if there were others who shared my concerns."

"So, basically, you've been talking behind Paul's back?" asked Frank.

"Look, it isn't that way!" Gracie objected. "I just needed to process my thoughts with some people. It wasn't like I was spreading rumors or anything."

Paul slowly shook his head. "Gracie, if the things you've been saying behind my back are true, then at best they can be classified as gossip. If they're not true, then at worst they can be classified as slander. Either way, it's a bad deal and toxic to the life of our church."

Gracie looked stunned. "I . . . I just didn't think of it that way." Tears began to pour down her face. "I don't even know what I can say."

Paul's anger went from a boil to a simmer. "Gracie, I think we'd better schedule a separate time to talk again, maybe in a few days. I need to think about this and so do you."

Gracie nodded and stood to leave. She looked at Frank. "I'm sorry, Frank. I've been really reckless in calling you about all of this." She looked over at Paul again. "I'm going home. And Paul, I think Frank's right. I need to step down from my leadership role."

"We'll talk about that in a few days, Gracie," said Paul.

After they were sure both Gracie and Ralph were gone, Frank and Paul sat back down. "Frank, you really took me by surprise. I figured we would have to play nice and try to be understanding and kind, as church people are supposed to be. You even said 'hell'!"

Frank chuckled. "Yeah, I guess I did. I'm sure that'll give Ralph something to talk about. Look—I'm just getting too old to put up with this kind of nonsense. Church seems to be a place where people try to wield power in ways that they can't anywhere else in their lives. Ralph is mad at the world and you are his choice in scapegoats. I'd be willing to bet that Gracie has been having her own religious biases challenged by you, and her friendship with Ralph's wife has made it easy for Ralph to find a vulnerable place in Gracie's mind. People like Ralph have radar for that kind of thing."

"Well, you sure short-circuited this whole deal." Paul frowned. "But who knows what Gracie has now stirred up in the church with all of her 'processing.'"

The Bartender

"That's going to be a tough one, Paul," said Frank. "It's hard to tell what the effects of Gracie's conversations will be. You can bet that some people just go on and don't give a thought to what she's been saying. But there are going to be others who will now start harboring their own doubts. This needs to be a serious area of prayer for us." Frank adjusted his suit coat and leaned forward so that he had Paul's attention. "Paul, the theological stuff is your department. I trust you in all that because I've come to love you as a pastor and friend. But let me give you this advice, whether you asked for it or not: If you think you've got something we need to know, then hit us directly and confidently. Show us how to read the scriptures so that we understand what you're talking about. Help us to buy in by showing us how to buy in to whatever it is God is up to. But whatever you do, don't just trickle your thought processes into our heads. Be courageous! We trust you—so go for it! If you're out in left field, then God will show us."

Paul smiled at Frank's wisdom. "OK, Frank. I'm taking your advice. Thanks."

They both stood to leave. "Just remember, Paul. If the church succeeds—whatever that means—then we give God the credit. If it fails, then it's all your fault. Isn't that just a great deal?"

Frank and Paul laughed. But Paul knew there was more truth in that statement than there was irony.

24

The love of God is greater far
Than tongue or pen can ever tell;
It goes beyond the highest star
And reaches to the lowest hell.

F. M. Lehman

When Angie arrived home from work it was 9:00. As she entered the apartment, one roommate was just leaving to meet her boyfriend. The other would not be returning from her job until close to midnight. Angie had the place to herself for a while.

As she sorted some things from her purse she found the paper Emil had given her that morning. *Me, Why?,* and *God.* She really just wanted to move robotically through the next few days and get this whole thing over with. Doing what Emil asked of her just made her think more about the sadness of her life than she wanted. But Emil had been such a good friend to her that she thought she probably owed it to him to go through with this little exercise. Besides, it probably wouldn't take all that long to do.

Angie roamed through the kitchen looking for something to eat. While she snacked on crackers and an apple, she thought about how Emil had instructed her: *Write one or two things that you want in life.* What did she really want? Was it a better job? New friends? A career path? A boyfriend? She guessed there was nothing wrong with those possibilities, but each of them seemed to drop like deadweights on the ground as she thought of them. They all seemed like a recycling of her life as it had been up to this point. She shook her head and saw a neon sign in her mind: *Same crap, different day.* No, those were not the things she really wanted.

She knew she wanted something more but couldn't exactly land on what that was. Angie thought about her family; she thought about Brian. If she could change all that had happened, what would she want?

I want my mom to love me so much that she doesn't kill herself.

I want my dad to love me so much that he does anything he can to keep me with him.

I want grandma and grandpa to love me so much that they act like they're glad I'm with them.

I want my sister to love me and for me to love her.

I want Brian to love me enough to care about what's happening to me and his baby.

Angie sat down at the kitchen table and held Emil's paper in her hands, oblivious to the tears that were streaming from her eyes. She reached into her purse for a pen. She stared at the paper for a little while, holding the pen expectantly. Her heart was pounding in her chest as though she were preparing to parachute out of an airplane for the first time. She felt that writing down what she really wanted out of life would actually make something happen. Then, in the first column of the paper she slowly wrote the words that described the single thing—the only thing—she knew she wanted more than anything else.

I want to be loved.

When Emil saw Angie leave work he wondered how her night would go. Would she do what he had asked of her? He knew the chance was great that she wouldn't. He recalled how hard it had been for him to do that when Father Tom had walked him through the process years ago. He remembered being angry as he wrote—listing all the things he wanted out of life and then blaming himself and everyone else for these things always seeming to elude his grasp. But after he settled down and actually invited God into the process—asking God what God believed about him!—something began to change.

Emil didn't have to close the pub so he headed for home just after Angie left. The evening was clear and pleasant, helping the noise and verbal traffic to become quiet in his head. When he walked into his tiny apartment, it was almost 9:30.

He showered and put on clean sweats and a t-shirt—his typical attire for his yoga workout. But there would be no workout tonight. This night felt like it would be more of a vigil. He brought his candle from the kitchen cabinet and placed it on a saucer in the middle of the floor. He lit

Chapter Twenty-four

the candle and then seated himself before it. As he settled into the lotus position, he breathed deeply, whispering quietly with each breath.

Lord Jesus, Son of God, have mercy on me.

Emil repeated that ancient prayer over and over, centering his mind on God. Over the years Father Tom taught him about the sacred practices of faith—spiritual disciplines—and how those practices served to bring people into a place of availability to God. So Emil learned about simple things like reading the Bible and praying for a few minutes each day. But then Father Tom showed him so many other ways to engage with God— quiet and solitude, hospitality toward others, worshipping God alone and with other people, reflection on God's presence in each day, fasting, and generosity. Father Tom claimed that these weren't just things that people did because they were so holy; they were things people did intentionally and sometimes even reluctantly because they desired to know God.

At first Emil experimented with some of these practices because he thought that somehow God would like him better if he did those things. In those days he was still carrying some guilt and regret over his misspent life, so currying God's favor seemed like a good idea. Father Tom seemed to expect that to happen and spent a great deal of time helping Emil to see something new: God had always loved him, and nothing Emil could do would make God love him more. For Emil, this was almost too much to take in. But, over time, he did take it in. Now the sacred practices of faith served to draw his attention closely to this God of love. It was like moving closer to the heat of the fireplace in order to get warm.

On this night Emil came to God not for his own sake, but for Angie's. Emil knew what a crucial time this was for Angie and that she was, maybe for the first time, looking at her life with the idea that God was a possibility. So Emil would come to God with the weight he carried for Angie.

What Emil wanted more than anything right now was sleep. It had been a long day and he was tired. So he knew that what he needed was to give up what he wanted for awhile—in a way, to *fast* from sleep—and center himself on God. He would keep sleep at bay for the time being. He began to pray.

Lord Jesus, Son of God, have mercy on me.

The Bartender

Angie was frightened by her uncontrolled weeping. She hadn't expected this at all. Yet, even as her body convulsed with her sobbing, she realized she had finally seen that for which her heart had always been longing: To be loved.

Love is what had always eluded her. Any memory of love from her mother was obscured by the act of self-destruction that had shown Angie that Mom preferred death to a life with her own children. Her father's halting attempts at love were really more like care-giving. Even that terminated when he dumped her and her sister. No one in her life—parents, grandparents, boyfriends or lovers—gave Angie even the suggestion that she was worthy of being loved.

She wondered, *Why hasn't this happened for me? It seems to happen for other people. It happens in movies. They must get it from somewhere.*

Angie's crying subsided enough for her to refocus her eyes on the paper lying before her. She had written down what she wanted. Now she needed to write something about why this had not happened in her life. She gripped the pen tightly and began to slowly shake her head as she wrote.

I was a bratty kid.
My sister and I were a pain to my grandparents.
I'm too stupid to pick guys who will treat me right.
I've screwed up my life so much that I don't deserve to be loved.

She could feel herself becoming angry. She believed that this was all her fault. If she hadn't been such an idiot then her life would have been better. Stupid people like her, she reasoned, didn't deserve any better. Angie could taste the bitterness in her mouth, as if it had invaded her whole body.

It was time to get this over with. There was still one more thing to do, according to Emil. She didn't know if she could really do this. At this point it seemed futile to her. She knew more than she wanted and her life's picture didn't look any prettier than it did before. The only difference was that now she felt more angry than sad.

Angie thought, *I'm not going to do this God-thing. Maybe that's OK for Emil, but it isn't going to change anything for me. I'm done with this.*

She wadded the paper into a ball and pushed it across the table. She got up from her chair and started cleaning up the dishes.

Chapter Twenty-four

Emil repeated his prayer like a mantra: *Lord Jesus, Son of God, have mercy on me.* If he had ever felt in need of God's mercy, it was now. He wondered what had he gotten himself into. His desire to help Angie see where God was in her life had escalated into his being a chauffeur to an abortion clinic. He asked himself if he had now become complicit in the death of Angie's unborn child. He thought about what it might mean to get so close to someone like Angie that you lose perspective and get their broken lives—their sin—all over you. What did God think of that?

Emil struggled to bring his mind to rest so that he could become centered and quiet.

I got your brokenness and sin all over me, Emil.

Emil caught his breath. He had learned to recognize this process. The thought would just stream into his mind as though someone was pouring words into an opening in his head through a funnel. He waited again.

I have Angie's brokenness and sin all over me.

During Emil's early days of recovery, Father Tom had encouraged him to memorize a verse from the Bible that he thought would help Emil when he felt like he was slipping back into the siren song of his addiction. It was Isaiah 53:4, and Emil had replayed it in his mind many times over the years.

> *Surely he has borne our infirmities and carried our diseases; yet we accounted him stricken, struck down by God, and afflicted.*

Emil knew that Christians had come to see this as a reference to Jesus. In Jesus they saw that somehow God himself had gotten the world's sin all over him and carried it to the place of death. Yet, even when people saw that possibility, they dismissed it as something God would never condescend to do. That's why so many of Jesus' countrymen rejected him: No one could be from God and die a sinner's death on a Roman cross. But it was just the opposite. God got the world's sin all over him and took it to the place of rejection, pain, and death.

Suddenly Emil knew that he did not have the power to endorse anyone's sin. All he knew to do was to follow Jesus, who had borne Emil's infirmities and carried his disease.

All at once he realized that he needed to pray for Angie. Emil felt a sense of struggle in his own heart and he knew it was for her. He felt like the friends who had taken their paralyzed friend to be healed by Jesus. In that biblical account, Jesus saw their faith and healed the man, who didn't seem to even be conscious. Emil would now approach God as Angie's friend. He hoped God would see his faith on behalf of his friend.

Lord Jesus, Son of God, have mercy on Angie.

As the water caressed her hands, Angie felt her anger subside. It was like the warm dishwater was soothing her heart as well as her hands. She thought again about Emil's instruction to her.

If you ask God to come, he'll come . . . Try it and see what happens . . . Maybe you'll find something out about how God heals self-inflicted wounds . . .

Without finishing the dishes, Angie carefully dried her hands on a paper towel. As she did, she walked slowly back to the table and looked at the crumpled ball of paper that lay before her. She tossed the towel on the table, sat down, and reached for the mangled sheet. As she unfolded it, she attempted to press the wrinkles out of it with her hands. She almost hoped it would be unreadable. The words remained clear.

Angie looked at the heading of the third column of the paper. *God.* Emil told her to ask God what he thought of all this. He said God would come if she asked. Angie asked herself what she would do if she actually heard something in her head. Even worse, she wondered: *What if I hear something in my head and find out God agrees with the mess I've made of my life?*

Her hands moved hesitantly from the table to her lap. She folded them not only out of a sense of religious protocol but also to keep them from shaking. Angie closed her eyes and prayed silently in her head: *God, what do you believe about me?*

Angie waited in silence, hearing nothing but the sound of a quiet breeze in her mind. It felt like a warm, sweet breath that brought peace.

Emil began to feel desperate. He feared that Angie might crash and burn emotionally because of his conversations with her. He had come to love

Chapter Twenty-four

Angie, not in a romantic way, but in a way that made him want to rescue her from her despair.

I have loved Angie long before you came on the scene, Emil, just as I have always loved you.

Emil relaxed his breathing and gave a nod to his head in assent to the words he had heard in his mind. He would trust Angie to the God who had always loved her.

Lord Jesus, Son of God, have mercy on us.

The first words Angie heard just seemed to appear in her mind.

I love you, Angie.

She was startled at first. Was this what Emil was talking about? She didn't trust her own mind. She could easily accept the idea that she was just talking to herself.

I have always loved you, Angie.

Angie's attention turned when she heard these words. She wouldn't talk to herself that way. Was this really happening? Was God actually talking to her? She began to tremble. She squeezed her hands together more tightly. She silently asked, *Are you really talking to me, God?*

When no one loved you, I loved you. And I love you now.

Once again her body began to shake. Angie cried out loud, covering her mouth with both hands. The tears coursed through her fingers and splashed on the table. She laid her head on the hard surface of the wood and continued to cry. She remained that way for what seemed to her like an endless space of time. After a while she stopped shaking. Her crying continued, but less forcefully now.

Angie knew at that moment that someone—the most important Someone—loved her. She would never have offered herself that possibility, which is what made this experience so real to her. She felt no accusations from God, no blame or fixing of guilt because of her own unworthiness. All she felt was acceptance and love.

Angie would later describe to Emil what happened next not as a vision but as a kind of waking dream. She was in the elevator again and it was racing toward its explosive end. But this time, even as she gripped the side railing, she forced herself to turn and look behind her. The motion reminded her of what she called "running dreams"—dreams where a person is trying to escape an attacker, only to find they are running as though they are waist high in mud. She fought to keep turning around, her anxiety mounting as she did so.

What she finally saw she could never clearly describe. All she knew was that she looked into eyes that were filled with nothing but love. At first she thought she was seeing Emil, but it was not him—it was someone *more*. It was like the care and kindness she had experienced in Emil was now more real and clear than she would ever have imagined. If Emil was good, then this was the One who gave him that goodness. In that moment she knew she was safe. The howling sound of the careening elevator dimmed as though a volume control was gradually turned to the *off* position. As the arms of this presence embraced her she knew she was no longer alone. She felt the terror and loneliness leak out of her life. The warmth of comfort and care washed over her and she melted into the One who held her so closely.

Angie could not say that she had come to understand love—she had been overwhelmed by it. But she knew that love wasn't what she thought—it wasn't just emotion or satisfaction or even acceptance. It was a person. This person—this love—had put his arms around her and drawn her close. They were arms that seemed just right for her and yet she seemed to recognize that they were endless in their reach. They were arms that extended far beyond her.

This was love. *She* was loved. Love had been given to her as she had always wanted. A thought floated lightly to the surface of her mind: *Maybe I can love.*

And this time, as the dream ended, the elevator did not crash. There was only a tender silence.

Emil's body jerked as if waking abruptly from sleep. He opened his eyes, looked around the room, and stretched his back. A sense of peace settled on him. He would sleep now.

25

Love never ends.

1 Corinthians 13:8

When Paul returned home, Sheila was just finishing up a phone call with her mother. After she hung up, she turned to Paul with her arms crossed. "So—are we fired?"

Paul dropped his car keys on the dining room table. "No, not fired. Just demoted. I'm now the associate pastor in charge of heresy."

Sheila gave him her best I'm-going-to-hurt-you look. "Paul! Really—what happened?"

"Well, when Gracie showed up she didn't come alone. She had Ralph Bennett with her, and ..."

"Ralph Bennett!" Sheila was outraged. "No way! What is wrong with her?"

"It's OK, Sheila. I think Gracie ended up really regretting her decision to bring him." Paul went on to give a concise account of the meeting, pausing only to let Sheila punctuate his summary with murderous threats against Ralph and Gracie.

When Paul was finished, Sheila was shaking her head and looking at the floor. "You know, as awful as this is, maybe there is something good happening in the middle of it. Frank's advice was really helpful—you've been thinking and talking about a new direction for our church, yet you've been hesitant to act. Maybe now is the time to lead decisively and help people to take the next step forward, whatever that is. It's kind of scary, but I think Frank's right."

Paul nodded in agreement. "Yeah, I think so, too. This makes me think of Emil, who just doesn't seem to get too bogged down in over-analysis like I do. He just trusts that God is at work and then jumps in. I think it's time that I jumped in."

"I think people are probably waiting for that, Paul. You know that I'm with you." Sheila's eyes began to glisten.

"I know you are, babe." Paul reached out for her and they embraced. Just as their lips met in what Paul began to hope would be the beginning of something even more wonderful, they heard footsteps halting at the door leading to the kitchen.

"Ugh. Gross. I'm going back to my room." Tyler disappeared as quickly as he had appeared.

"Why is it that kids think their parents are sexual zombies?" asked Paul. "How do they think they got here in the first place?"

Sheila wrinkled her forehead in thought. "Try to imagine your own parents for a moment..."

"Arrggh! OK, OK, I get it. No more images, please!"

Sheila smiled in an inviting way. "Any more images in there?"

Paul looked around. "I just want to make sure Tyler is gone." They returned to where they were before they were interrupted.

Paul lay awake long after Sheila had gone to sleep. He couldn't stop thinking about how he might take all that had been percolating through his mind and translate it into something that could be communicated to the people of his church. He also wondered how he was going to tell Sheila that Gracie had been salting members of the church with all of her doubts about him. Sheila would be overwhelmed by the prospect of having some kind of mob scene at church. Actually, Paul realized that *he* was overwhelmed by it all. He had never had to deal with mass accusations and he didn't know if he could now. Paul had to remind himself that he didn't even know that the problem was as big as he feared. But he still feared it.

Paul realized that he could really lose everything. If Frank was any indication of the board's support of him, he wasn't in danger of being fired. But the people of the church could vote with their feet. He could find himself without a sustainable congregation and without a job.

He felt like new things were going to start happening for him—not in terms of church busyness, but rather inside of him, in his own inner life with God. Paul was excited, but he wondered how that would look as he learned how to have an outward life that made a difference in his own world—even if that world got messy.

Paul thought again of Emil and how willing he seemed to be to accept and reach out to the people around him, regardless of their messi-

Chapter Twenty-five

ness. Emil had gone through his own kind of hell with alcoholism. That seemed to create an openness to others that might be more difficult for people like Paul.

That's why followers of Jesus can engage in the messiness of going with God's Spirit into the world. That's why people like me don't need to be ashamed of being with the broken and hurting—and even the downright sinful—of the world. It's because all their brokenness, pain, and sin are also part of who I am. Yes, there is forgiveness in Jesus. Yes, God's Spirit gives strength and release from the power of sin. But the possibilities are all there. While I might not do some of the horrible things others might do, the possibilities and potential for that horror are still there. That's why I never have the right to be judgmental.

So does that mean that a Christian's life of spiritual formation should lead to just hanging around with people and smiling at their destructive lives, hoping that they'll finally catch on to what God wants for them? No, but it does mean that my own life, centered in Christ, should result in a realistic assessment of myself rather than an elevation of myself. So I can be freed to embrace people as true brothers and sisters, not to stand by passively while they destroy themselves, but instead to stand with them compassionately, helping them to see how God has already loved them and that God is already present and at work in their lives.

Paul felt sleep finally coming toward him. As he closed his eyes, he prayed:

God, I want to keep going deeper in this journey with you. I want to really know you. And I want to go where your Spirit leads me—into the hurting, lonely places of the world. Thank you for the help I found in Emil. Bless him as he walks this out in his own life. And rescue me from the fear of loss that has captured me.

26

*No one has greater love than this,
to lay down one's life for one's friends.*

John 15:13

WHEN EMIL CAME INTO the pub on Wednesday morning to start his shift he looked for Angie but didn't see her. He checked the work schedule and saw that she was supposed to be there. He began to worry that something was wrong. He checked with Bobby, the pub manager who was in the office sorting out invoices.

"Bobby—have you heard from Angie? She's supposed to be here today." Emil tried to sound casual.

"Yeah, she came in when I first opened up this morning. She said she wasn't feeling well and had a doctor's appointment or something tomorrow. She looked pretty wrung out to me. Probably had a rough night!" Bobby chuckled and shook his head. It wasn't unusual for some of the employees to fight hangovers when they arrived at work. It wouldn't have been the first time for Angie. Bobby reached over to a stack on his desk and grabbed a small envelope and handed it to Emil.

"Here—I almost forgot. She left this note for you. Not getting in over your head here, are you buddy?"

Emil took the note. "No, don't worry about me. Thanks." Emil wandered back out toward the bar. He slipped behind it and slowly tore open the envelope. He read the note to himself:

Emil,

I did the things last night on the paper you gave me. I think something happened for me, but I'm not really ready to talk about it. I need some time. I need to get some of my stuff out of the way before I can really think clearly. But I think it's going to be OK.

My appointment at the clinic got moved up. It's tomorrow morning at 8:00. I needed to go in today for some preliminary stuff. I know it's short notice, but can you still take me? I saw that you don't work tomorrow, so I

Chapter Twenty-six

hope I'm not wrecking your day off. Will you give me a call and let me know if this works for you?

Angie

Emil folded the note and put in his pocket. He started reorganizing the glasses under the bar and then checked the beer taps. After a few minutes he retrieved the note and looked at it again. He took out his cell phone and punched in the number Angie had scrawled at the bottom of the paper. He heard it ringing.

"Hello?"

"Hi Angie, it's Emil."

"Hi, Emil. You got my note."

"Yeah, I did. I can take you tomorrow. What time do you want me to pick you up?"

"Thanks so much, Emil. Can you get me at 7:30?"

"Sure. I'll be there."

Angie was quiet for a moment. "Thanks again." Her voice was soft.

Emil felt a tightening in his throat. "It's OK. I'll see you tomorrow, Angie."

After he turned off his phone, Emil went back to work. His mind could only swirl around one repetitious phrase:

Lord Jesus, Son of God, have mercy on us.

27

As he came near and saw the city, he wept over it.

Luke 19:41

THE RECEPTIONIST AT THE family planning clinic finished making the morning coffee and retrieving the messages from the phone answering system. She had plans for the weekend and was glad it was Friday because the clinic always closed early at the end of the week. As she thought about the pleasure of a shorter work day she looked over the morning appointment sheet.

Just a few minutes later the buzzer on the door rang, signaling the arrival of the first patient. She looked at the screen on the security system. Yes, she remembered this one from yesterday. The girl would be in and out in no time. This must be the "friend" she said she would bring so that she wouldn't have to drive herself home. There was another buzz as the receptionist released the security lock on the door.

As the couple entered, the man took a seat in the waiting area while the girl approached the window made of thick, protective glass. The receptionist sized up the situation in her own mind: *An older guy—cute, but a lot older than the girl. Another inconvenient knock-up.* She'd seen it a million times. She logged in the girl's name and pressed the button that would open the door into the procedure rooms. The girl entered and disappeared down the hallway.

The receptionist stole another look at the man in the waiting area. He didn't seem nervous like the others who brought their women in. This one looked sad, like he was carrying a really heavy weight. *Guilt will do that*, she thought.

She went back to her work. She didn't look up at the man again for twenty or thirty minutes. She didn't notice that his lips were barely moving as though he were speaking secretly to someone. She didn't see the tear that found its way down his face.

28

*I turned and gave my heart up to despair concerning
all the toil of my labors under the sun.*

Ecclesiastes 2:20

Angie sat on the edge of the examination table. She began to tremble, as much from anxiety as from the cool temperature. In the early morning quiet of the clinic the small room felt like a vault to her.

Only a few hours ago she experienced something entirely new to her. Having the feeling that God was somehow speaking to her had to bring some kind of change into her life. She just didn't know what that change would be. She remembered feeling peaceful and accepted in those moments at her kitchen table. But now she felt very alone and frightened again.

Closing her eyes, Angie hoped to calm herself before the doctor came in. An image appeared in her mind: The elevator. She shuddered, fearing that the vision of falling and crashing was about to return. Angie almost opened her eyes, but she stopped herself. She wanted to see if anything was about to happen.

Something was different. The elevator she saw in her mind wasn't moving. She saw herself first in the elevator as one might see someone through a security camera. Then she realized that the perspective had changed—she was now looking through her own eyes.

Angie looked around. It was the same little enclosure with the same wood paneling and brass fittings. She was alone this time. There was no anonymous presence standing behind her. She began to fear that the vision would end here.

She studied the panel of buttons next to the door. There were many—it appeared to be a tall building. Yet the rows and rows of buttons weren't numbered. She pushed one, then the other. Nothing happened. Once again her fear of ending in this isolation came alive.

At the bottom of the panels were the typical buttons that would either close or open the doors. Angie stared at the button labeled "open."

What if I push it and nothing happens? Even worse, what if something does happen?

Angie thought for a moment. *It seems like I've always been a victim of life. Things just keep happening to me and then I do things and just keep letting more things happen to me. But I've taken some risks lately—risks in talking to Emil, risks in talking to God like I was a crazy person. It feels like new things might be happening with me instead of to me. Maybe I'll take one more risk.*

She tentatively reached out her hand. Her finger hovered over the button. She pressed it.

At first nothing happened. Her heart sank. That suffocating feeling of aloneness began to surround her again. Then the elevator shuddered and the doors began to separate. Light poured into the space. Strangely, it wasn't light from artificial sources. It was sunlight.

Angie looked out and saw a grassy area divided by a curving brick walkway. There were two trees, one on each side of the walkway, their branches creating a leafy canopy. Flowers were blooming at the base of the trees. She stepped out of the elevator and onto the grass.

The freshness of the air startled her. She hadn't realized how stuffy the elevator had been. She breathed deeply, feeling refreshment flood into her. The brick walkway curved through the grassy space and ran right underneath the elevator. Angie was standing on the bricks now. She took a few steps forward.

Angie turned back to look at the elevator. It was gone. There was no indentation on the grass that would suggest anything had ever been there. The path continued to run past where the elevator had been and ran into the distance. She turned back toward the two trees.

As she walked a sense of familiarity struck her. She was sure she had never been to this place before. It was too beautiful. She was sure she would have remembered it. As she walked she felt her anticipation rising. Yes, this place was familiar even if she didn't know why.

Angie passed the trees, lifting her face as the sunlight drifted through the lacy branches. A light breeze caused a stir in the leaves that sounded like water flowing through a stream. She felt alive and new. She closed her eyes and let the sensory experience of this place take over.

The sensation of the unfiltered sunlight signaled Angie's movement through the trees. She opened her eyes and looked ahead. She stopped on the path. Before her was a small house—more of a cottage, actually. It

Chapter Twenty-eight

was made of dark wood and had a gently sloping roof with shingles that wrapped around the eaves, creating a soft, flowing effect. She noticed a brick chimney at the peak of the roof. Wisps of smoke escaped from the top. Three stone steps lifted from the brick path up to a porch that ran the length of the front of the cottage. Two posts made of melon-sized stones held up the roof over the porch. Angie could see a single rocking chair sitting between the front door and a large paned window. A small side table sat to the left of the chair, a bouquet of flowers in a vase standing on its surface. The front door was large with a small window of leaded glass at the top. The door was painted barn red. She saw that the handle was made of ornate wrought iron.

Angie stood still staring at the house. She felt as though time had stopped and all of life had become focused on this moment. She was aware of tears running down her face. To her, this was the most beautiful place she had ever seen. The familiarity of the scene still puzzled her but did not diminish her rising awareness that she belonged here. All at once she understood why.

She was home.

Angie was startled by the sound of a door handle turning. The vision of the cottage disappeared. She opened her eyes and once again saw the sterile examination room. The door of the room pushed open and a white-coated lab technician entered. He smiled at her and then stopped, seeing the tears on her face. "I'm sorry. Do you need a few minutes?"

Angie wiped her face with her hands. "Yes, please. Just a few."

29

There is no fear in love, but perfect love casts out fear.

1 John 4:18

THE DOOR CLICKED LOUDLY as Angie opened it. She stepped into the waiting room and looked toward Emil. Emil lifted his head and looked up in surprise. He hadn't expected her so soon. Of course, he didn't know much about these procedures except that they had become pretty routine. It figured that they would also be quick.

Angie looked alright, except that her eyes were a little red. She also seemed peaceful. Emil wondered how the accomplishment of this sad goal would impact her already broken life.

As Angie walked toward Emil she saw him wipe his face, as though he had been crying. She recognized sadness in his face, but she saw something else. It wasn't rejection, as she had experienced so often in her life. It wasn't disgust or anger. It was something familiar yet new, something she had only experienced in an authentic way during her unbelievable experience last night.

It was love.

She felt no sense of the erotic in this love. It was a love that felt like the love that poured out of those eyes that so captured her as she melted down in her apartment. It was a love that compelled a person to suffer with another person in a deeply painful place. Angie couldn't find judgment or condemnation in Emil's eyes. Instead it was something that she was beginning to recognize and something she felt she might even be capable of herself.

It was love.

"Emil, let's go. I'm ready to go home."

30

I saw all the deeds that are done under the sun; and see, all is vanity and a chasing after wind. What is crooked cannot be made straight, and what is lacking cannot be counted.

Ecclesiastes 1:14–15

PAUL WAS GLAD IT was Friday morning. Fridays were his days for getting fully prepared for Sundays. He enjoyed the time of quiet, prayer, study, and writing. He usually checked his emails first thing, but then he didn't return to them until the end of the day.

Included among the dozen or so email messages in his inbox was one from Gracie. He supposed she was initiating a meeting time with him.

He was wrong.

> Paul,
>
> I just found out from my boss that my next assignment is in New York. I'll be leaving Monday morning and will be gone for several weeks—maybe even a couple of months. Maybe this is going to work out for the best.
>
> I've been giving a lot of thought to what happened Tuesday night. Again, I'm sorry about the way I handled this. I think I let Ralph into this whole thing because I was feeling angry and afraid of what I felt like you were doing. I'm just sorry.
>
> I'm going to formally resign from the leadership team. I will explain that my work demands are going to make me inaccessible for awhile—I think people will understand that.
>
> This time that I'll be gone will help me sort out a lot of things, like whether or not I really should continue with Music City. I'm not sure I fit anymore. There are just too many things that I'm uncomfortable with. It's most likely my problem, but it's there nevertheless.
>
> Maybe we can talk some by email during my trip. On the other hand, it just might be good to create some space here.
>
> Gracie

31

"For this reason I tell you that her sins, many as they are,
have been forgiven her,
because she has shown such great love."

Luke 7:47

EMIL OPENED THE CAR door for Angie, nervous about how to help her. He couldn't imagine what she was feeling, both physically and emotionally. As he took her arm to help her into the car, Angie glanced up at him and smiled with a look that spoke to Emil more of amused affection than of painful gratitude. He didn't understand how the weight of what just happened could be so heavy for him when Angie seemed to be at ease. He thought that maybe she was convincing herself that she had just solved a significant problem and was feeling a sense of temporary relief.

As they pulled away from the clinic, Emil began to offer a word of comfort and then stopped, realizing that silence was probably more appropriate. After a few minutes he gave into his own anxiety and asked, "Angie, how are you feeling?"

Angie remained quiet for several seconds then responded, "I'm OK."

Emil was puzzled. "Did they give you some medication for pain or anything?"

"Emil, really—I'm OK."

"Angie, you've been through a physical ordeal here. I'm just concerned that . . ."

Angie reached over and gently gripped Emil's arm. "Emil, I just need a little space, alright?"

He looked at her face and saw that she wasn't angry, but distant in a way that suggested something was being processed deep in her mind. He turned his eyes back to the road and nodded.

As they approached Angie's neighborhood, Emil spoke again. "Angie . . ."

"Emil—some space, *please?*"

Chapter Thirty-one

He admitted defeat to himself. Emil felt that he had learned so much about being attentive to people, listening to their stories, and then helping them to see the possibility of God in their lives. Yet, here he was, sitting right next to someone who had trusted him and invited him into a very difficult life event, and he was coming away confused. Now *he* was wondering where God was in all of this.

Emil stopped the car at the curb in front of Angie's apartment. He was ready to ask her if he could help her inside, then thought better of it. Angie wanted space, so she would have to ask for what she needed. They sat quietly in the car. Angie seemed to be looking off in the distance. Finally she spoke.

"You know that Father Tom guy you told me about?"

"Sure. My mentor."

"Would you take me to talk to him?"

Emil was surprised but also happy to hear that Angie wanted some guidance. Father Tom would be a great post-abortion counselor. "Of course I will. Angie, I think this is a really good . . ."

He stopped in mid-sentence as Angie fixed him with a glare. "Emil! *Space!*" Her face softened to a gentle smile. "Do you think he's available now?"

Emil nodded. He figured Father Tom would make time in his day for Angie. He started the car and pulled away, wondering what was about to happen.

Epilogue

The best way to know God is to love many things.

Vincent van Gogh

It had been six months since Paul, Dean, and Gracie started their conversation about evangelism. New things were, indeed, happening in Paul's life. Lindsay was getting ready to start college and would be moving to the dorm soon. It was only a two-hour drive to the campus, but Paul and Sheila were already struggling with the impending empty nest syndrome, even though Tyler still had two years to go before he graduated from high school.

Gracie disappeared from the life of Music City. During her extended business trip Paul emailed her a few times but only received cursory responses indicating that she was fine and very busy with her consulting assignment. At the end of that assignment she accepted a promotion and transfer to New York City. She contacted several friends she had at the church to let them know what was happening, but she never contacted Paul.

Paul had experienced this kind of thing before and it never happened without pain. It amazed him how people could share so much together in their common life of worship and community, yet disappear overnight when things didn't suit them. He knew there were complex emotions wrapped up in these kinds of departures but the abruptness and sense of dismissal were sometimes overwhelming. Paul grieved at the loss of Gracie.

Dean was flourishing in his studies at the seminary and also began to develop quite a following among the college-aged young people in the community. He started to meet on Sunday nights with a number of them at a local café where he led an open discussion about the big questions of life and faith. Paul and Dean continued to work closely together, and Paul was appreciative of Dean's contribution to the life of the church. Paul hoped that Dean would stay with the church for a long time, but he expected that Dean would launch his own church one day. That would test Paul's willingness to give away the best of the church, but he believed that God really preferred it that way.

For the most part, the leadership team of the church had been receptive to the ideas and recommendations that Paul brought. Paul avoided bringing in a top-down plan that would simply impose his own ideas on everyone. Instead, he asked the team to build a new direction for the church. He was pleased at their willingness to entertain new things, but was somewhat surprised at their hesitation in letting the new things begin with them. Paul told the team that any new focus in the church that would have to do with inward transformation would have to start with the leadership team. They would have to take their own spiritual formation more seriously than ever before. They would need to make commitments to one another and hold one another accountable for their intentional life of devotion. While the team members struggled with their own commitments, they finally agreed that this was the only way to move forward. They got excited about the possibilities that God might bring. Only one team member—one who served on the board of directors—dissented from the process. In fact, he resigned from the board, stating "personal time constraints" as the reason for his inability to continue in leadership. Paul knew that the man was struggling with his own faith and other life issues. This just wouldn't be the right time for him to serve as a leader—for his sake and for the sake of the church.

Paul began to speak on Sundays more and more about how people might orient their lives around God. He introduced them to the classic spiritual disciplines and showed how the Bible directs people to the richness of a life centered in God. He continued this emphasis in the weekly Bible study that he taught. It had been too easy for him to get lost in the historical background of the text or in the nuances of the original Hebrew or Greek language. Now he worked more to draw people into the text of scripture in such a way that they were challenged each week with the way they were ordering their own lives. Paul wasn't prescriptive or authoritative about this, but he did point the people to the reality of living out the implications of being a follower of Jesus. Attendance at the Bible study eroded, but the ones who remained seemed to be very serious about their own spiritual formation. Paul took comfort in that.

Paul taught a six-week series on Sundays about how the gospel—the good news—was Jesus' invitation into the kingdom of God. He showed how Jesus' death on the cross was how God showed that he was really *Emmanuel*—God *with* us—and that his kingdom had come into the real drama of human history. Jesus' death on the cross really was a rescue from sin and it was also a rescue from the exile away from God that sin brought. But Jesus' death wasn't just a transaction that got people into heaven. His death was proof that God gave all of himself for the human race. It was a breaking of the strangle-hold that sin had over people. And it was the prelude to resurrection, where new life could be had by all. It was, Paul reasoned, an old message. Yet, in many ways, it was new for followers of Jesus.

As Paul had feared, there were people who had been negatively affected by both Gracie and Ralph. Over the last six months the church lost almost thirty percent of its congregation. The departing families included people that Paul and Sheila had considered to be long-time friends. Some left with only an email message as their goodbye.

The leadership team stood staunchly behind Paul. Frank had done a great job in preparing them for the losses due simply to change if not because of negative influences. Frank reminded the team that, even in the world of business, making changes always results in some kind of exodus for those who struggle with change. The team agreed that they would follow Paul's leadership and help others to do the same. They would see themselves as a kind of remnant that would trust God and seek to obey him. They recognized that obedience would look like loving God and extending themselves to love others.

Paul knew that the church's engagement with other people would be a long process. He had become content with letting God unfold this part of the change. Two of his leadership team members began to share stories of developing new friendships—one with a neighbor and the other with a co-worker—and learning to see where God was working in those lives. Paul was thrilled to hear those stories and received them as tokens of what God might do among them.

There were still the faithful people of the church who continued to do what they had always considered to be obedience to God. Paul realized that he had taken for granted their stories of sharing God's love with the people of their own world. When he heard about someone praying with a person at work, or sharing their own life of faith with another person, or helping a neighbor in need, Paul started encouraging the people. He tried

Epilogue

to help them see how God was working in that person. They would pray together for these people. On occasion, Paul would even invite someone to share their story of relationship with the congregation during a Sunday service. He hoped that these stories would inspire others to stretch their faith beyond themselves.

A story that Paul would always remember came from a young woman who exercised daily on the walking path of a local park. She was somewhat introverted so her story of encounter was particularly impacting to those who heard it. Her own description during a Sunday gathering was the highpoint of the morning.

"I was doing my regular power walk at the park and I saw this woman sitting on one of the benches with her face covered by her hands. As I walked by I could hear her crying. I really didn't want to be intrusive so I just kept walking. Then I started thinking about what Paul's been teaching about living our lives in the reality of God's kingdom and looking for what God is doing in the people around us. I really felt like God was telling me to go back to that woman. I don't do that kind of thing naturally, so I figured it must be God urging me to get involved.

"If you know this park, then you might remember the guy who is always selling flowers right at the park entrance. I went to my car and got some money, then ran to the flower stand and bought a small bouquet. All the time, I kept praying that the woman would still be there.

"When I went back I saw that she was still there, now just staring off through the trees. I came up to her with the flowers and said (and this was really hard for me), 'I just thought you could use these today.' Well, the woman started crying again, even harder this time.

"I sat down with her and she told me that she was having a lot of trouble in her marriage and with her kids. She felt like a total failure and had even considered taking her own life. I told her I believed that, regardless of all our failures, God deeply loves us and wants something much better for us. I asked her if I could pray for her, and she said I could.

"When I finished, she hugged me and said I was an angel sent to save her. We exchanged phone numbers. I guess we'll just see what God has in mind next." Paul knew that this brief story of faithfulness and risk said more than any of his sermons could ever say.

One of Paul's greatest challenges was to reorient his own life toward God. He realized that his own life of devotion had become something that he fitted into the really *important* areas of his life—study, meetings, planning, and so on. Paul determined to change that and to see all the activities of his work as something that would flow out of what was truly important: His devotion to God.

This brought a challenge to Paul's work schedule. He had always prided himself on his early morning work ethic, often meeting with people from church or other pastors in the community for breakfast. Now he allowed only the most crucial of those meetings to interfere with his new morning regimen of prayer and meditation. Even when early meetings were necessary he began to rise earlier for prayer. Paul remembered reading a study indicating that pastors in the United States spend almost no time in personal prayer. He understood this as he struggled to make prayer a natural rhythm in his own life. He even went to the extent of programming both his laptop computer and his PDA to alert him just before lunch time so that he would stop, become aware of who and what was going on around him, and pray through a series of prayers from the Anglican *Book of Common Prayer*.

In addition to his new daily routines, Paul also scheduled a series of personal silent retreats for himself. One day a month he escaped to a beautiful Roman Catholic retreat center about an hour away from his home. During this time he prayed, wrote in his journal, read, and spent times of quiet roaming the grounds. He would sometimes fast and always took a short nap in one of the private rooms offered by the center.

These new practices served to jar Paul from his work life, which had become like a standard business life. At first he struggled with the time these practices took from his day, as though he was cheating his church by spending time with God. There was such irony in that mindset! During one of his retreat visits he spent an hour with an elderly priest named Father Donovan. After Paul shared his own struggles with being away from his office and regular duties, Father Donovan spoke out of his own lifetime experience of living a life of focused prayer:

"Son, prayer is your first work, not your last. Without giving yourself to God, your work will very likely be something that is only a reflection of *you*. I think you truly want your work to be a reflection of God. Prayer is the way you safeguard your vocation from yourself." It was as though God himself was speaking to him. At that moment he knew that this new and risky place of devotion had to be the primary activity of his life or he would never learn about who God had intended him to be.

Epilogue

Paul's busy life now kept him from his regular visits to the pub. In the past six months he had only been there two or three times, and each time he brought someone with him for a meeting or conversation. He only had minimal contact with Emil during that time. Then, one morning, Paul ran into Emil at *The Grinder*.

"Hey, Paul. Where have you been?" Emil appeared pleased to see Paul again.

Paul pulled up a chair and joined Emil at his table. "Man, I've been on quite a journey. I've been changing a lot of the way I do life and it's just thrown my routines into some uncharted territories."

Emil looked interested. "Really? What kind of changes?"

"Well, my work schedule is a bit different these days. We've experienced some fairly significant losses of people at church, so I've started teaching a couple of classes at a Christian college a few miles away. It helps with the loss of income."

"Wow," said Emil. "That's a pretty big change for you. Are you OK with it?"

"Yeah, actually I am," said Paul. "The teaching is fun and it really stretches me. Once I got used to the idea of getting my income from a variety of places it seemed like less of a failure than I'd expected."

Emil chuckled. "Hey, you're talking to a guy who's been tending bar for most of his life. It sounds great to me. How is your family doing with this change? It must be a little weird for them, too."

"At first it was. We all started wondering if maybe our little world was crashing in on us. But now that things have kind of stabilized I think we're alright with just being along for the ride for the time being."

"So, what has this done inside of you?" asked Emil.

"Well, I've been learning about centering my life in God more than in my work. I've been learning about prayer and quiet and various spiritual disciplines. I think it's all been really good, but it has changed the way I relate to my church. I think people see that change and wonder if it's permanent. I hope it is."

"Sounds like some pretty authentic stuff," said Emil. "So what else is going on?"

Paul thought for a moment. "I think the thing that I see in myself more than anything is that I'm more attentive. I'm attentive to God and I'm also more attentive to the people around me. I find an increasing expectation that God is doing something in everyone around me and I keep looking for what that is. Sometimes I feel like I must be completely obtuse on a spiritual level but every once in a while—and it's happening with greater frequency—I just feel confident that God is at work and I can actually talk to the person about what I see. When that has happened it's been an amazing experience."

"Wow. So something like this actually happened?"

"Well, yeah, it did. This really took me by surprise. A couple in my church was talking with me about how often they seemed to have hurt and broken young people landing on their doorsteps. They always took these kids in. Sometimes it would be a relative, other times a friend of one of their own children. They were getting a bit weary with the girl that was currently living in their guest bedroom and had come to me to talk about the situation. At one point the husband looked at me and said, 'We've been doing this kind of thing for a long time. It's like we're always being called to give and give to these kids. We're giving out but nothing is ever coming in. I know it sounds selfish, but I've been asking God when we're going to get *ours!*'

"Emil, it was weird. Before I could even think it through, the words seemed to just jump out of my mouth. I said, 'But this *is* yours.' The couple just stared at me. I said, 'You've been waiting for some kind of payback, as though the reward is something disconnected from what you are doing. The reward is realizing that you are up to your ears in doing what burns in God's heart.' The woman started to cry and the man was just dumbfounded. We talked about how what they did with these kids could be seen as a life calling rather than an intrusion. They got really excited. I think it's going to change the way they look at their whole life." Paul was beaming.

Emil asked, "Have you experienced this with anyone who doesn't seem to have any obvious God-connection?"

Paul looked down and shook his head. "No, I haven't. I believe in it as a possibility, but I'm not sure I've really got my mind around how that might happen. When you're talking to people in the church they expect to talk about God. It's not that way with others so it just seems awkward. I've been accustomed to transferring information about God to people when I've believed the time to be right, but not taking the risk to actually

Epilogue

suggest that God is already doing something. It's like I can't see the hook to hang those words on."

Emil said, "Maybe you don't need to see the hook. Maybe you just need to change the way you see people. It could be that you still see them as *ins* and *outs*; some people are *in* because they are in the church, or are Christians while everyone else is *out*. But don't we really believe that God's love is for everyone? Isn't that what Jesus was showing when he touched the untouchables and the outcasts?"

"So how does this really work, then?" Paul asked. "How does someone like me go about helping people see where God is when they aren't really oriented that way?"

"Get back into the pub business, amigo." Emil smiled. "Change the way you connect with your own world. Stop going to restaurants or office supply stores or wherever you go, strictly as a consumer. Go as a missionary. Look, you were coming to the pub for a long time, but you usually came because you liked doing your meetings there. Try going places with regularity and make some new friends with servers and clerks and all the people you engage with. Learn their names and start praying for them. Start asking them about their lives and listen to what they say. If you do that, then I believe you'll see more hooks than you know what to do with."

Paul nodded in understanding. "It sounds like a pretty long-term commitment."

"Paul, since when was following Jesus just another horse race? What do you care if it takes ten or twenty years for these processes to unfold? God's doing the work anyway, not us."

As Emil spoke, Paul felt a weight lift off of him. He realized that Emil was right: This life of faith was truly a *life* and not an *event*. It was a life of spiritual formation—of intentional devotion to God—and it was a life of following Jesus into the myriad of relationships that would unfold in the rhythms of everyday life. This was what it was like to live in God's love. That's what made his life make sense. That was how he could make sense of the activities of faith and the experience of faith. A phrase materialized in his mind: *God's love is the glue that binds being and doing together*. He would need to write that one down.

"You're right, Emil. This really helps me—thanks. I'm going to recharge my pub visits each week with a new way of looking at what's going on there. Maybe I'll even get a chance to connect with Angie. Hey—speaking of Angie—how's she doing? Is she still there?"

Emil thought for a moment as a smile found its way to his face. "No, she's not there anymore. But I still see her all the time."

Paul made arches out of his eyebrows. "Are you two in some kind of relationship?"

"Not in the way you're thinking, Paul." Emil chuckled. "Actually, Angie has really changed. You might be shocked at this, but she now lives in the guest house behind the rectory where Father Tom—my pastor—lives. She does some housecleaning for him and also helps him with some of his church work."

Paul was astonished. "You've got to be kidding me. What in the world happened?"

"Well, to make a long story short, she just got surprised by love. God did show up in her life and she started to see it. She learned about being loved and about being able to give love. Remember that scene in the Bible where the prostitute poured that expensive oil on Jesus and cried on his feet and all that? Didn't Jesus say that because she had so much forgiven in her life that she could now really love? I think it was kind of like that for Angie."

"Emil, are you saying that Angie is a Christian?"

Emil hesitated before answering. "Well, she's in process. Let me put it this way: If Jesus walked into the room, she'd know who he was."

Paul and Emil parted company and renewed their shared interest in getting together again. Paul assured Emil that he would see him regularly at the pub again. Emil gave him the thumbs-up as they separated, indicating his support of Paul's new adventure.

Emil needed to get back to Father Tom's house. The two of them had been as excited as a couple of kids as they worked through their plan to surprise Angie. She was away for a week at a retreat that Father Tom had recommended, and the two men had only three days left to accomplish their goal.

Epilogue

The women of the parish had been so great in gathering up the furniture that Angie needed. They conscripted their husbands—most of whom were retired—to repair and refinish each piece. The men took to it with masculine determination. While most of them would never admit it, they had a hard time hiding their new identities as knights in armor.

Emil and Father Tom had volunteered to do the painting. Emil hated painting, but threw himself into the project for Angie's sake. The focus was on the second of two bedrooms in the guest house. It was going to be great fun to see Angie's response when she got home.

When Emil arrived, Father Tom was already at work. Emil entered the guest house and found his way past the restored furniture pieces in the front room that were awaiting placement in the new room. As he stepped into the bedroom he began to laugh. Father Tom—now in overalls and t-shirt rather than his usual black clerical shirt and collar—had bright blue paint smeared across his forehead.

"Hey, Rembrandt. Planning to audition for the Blue Man Group?"

"Are you going to do a fashion critique or get over here and help me?" asked Father Tom.

Emil kept chuckling to himself as he gathered up his painting equipment in order to finish the trim around the doors. "Ok, Ok, don't panic. I'm here."

Standing back from the wall he had just completed, Father Tom looked on his own work with appreciation. "You don't think it's too bright, do you Emil?"

Emil stood next to Father Tom and put his arm around his shoulders. "Nope. I think it's great. Blue is a good brain-stimulating color, don't you think?"

Father Tom smiled and nodded in agreement. "Yup, it is. It's the perfect color for a nursery."

Chapter Comments

1. The description of Music City Church roughly parallels the church I planted in 1997. The church was located in Fullerton, California, where Fender guitars were invented and where Jackson Browne went to high school.

    My friend and co-grandparent Nancy shared the story with me of her journey of prayer with the student suffering from AIDS.

2. Dr. Grayson is actually a combination of two people: The head of the Religion department at the college where I was an undergraduate and my high school youth pastor who was the first to set me on a course of critical thinking and radical faith. Again, there is a personal parallel here. I did change my major and go into the field of education for six years. But I also went into the business world for another fourteen years before becoming a pastor.

3. The quotation by Dietrich Bonhoeffer is from *Life Together* (San Francisco: HarperSanFrancisco, 1978), 20.

    Over the last twenty or so years my church environment has looked like Paul's at Music City. But I still feel like God shows up more readily in old church buildings where they actually have to rub oil on the wood.

    Thank you to Leonard Sweet for revealing the sacramental nature of coffee.

4. The quotation by René Descartes is from *The Encyclopedia of Religious Quotations* (Westwood, New Jersey: Fleming H. Revell Company, 1965), 117.

    I was a regular at a local pub for eight years. I went almost every Tuesday for lunch. The environment of the pub and the friends I've made there have inspired much of my story.

5. A trusted friend from the pub has helped me to understand the value of recovery groups like Alcoholics Anonymous. My friend's honest spiritual journey has helped to form Emil's character. Angie is a combination of a number of young women whose stories of abandonment, abuse, and disappointment are all too common.

   Emil's drink-pouring that results in a leanness of the soul is a borrow from the *Book of Common Prayer* psalter:

   > *He gave them what they asked, but sent leanness into their soul.*
   > (Ps 106:15)

6. The quotation by Karl Barth is from The *Encyclopedia of Religious Quotations* (Westwood, New Jersey: Fleming H. Revell Company, 1965), 76.

   Susan Howatch's *Starbridge* series (New York: HarperCollins) was, for me, an intriguing and gritty look into broken human lives that find God's healing through relationships of spiritual direction.

7. The need for authenticity seemed to demand some occasional coarse language, but "hell" was the most I was willing to offer. As I recall, the word is found in the Bible.

8. This conversation was partially borrowed from one I had with a young man who was the president of the Atheists and Agnostics club at the local university.

9. A book that is read after 6:00 PM is, for me, a sleeping pill.

10. I have a friend at the pub who has found yoga to be both physically and spiritually healing.

11. A young woman who works at the pub shared this dream with me during one of my weekly lunches. She has kindly given me permission to put her dream into Angie's experience.

12. A special seminar on the atonement at Fuller Theological Seminary launched me on a new journey to find out what the good news is really about. I'm very grateful for that experience. Many thanks to Richard Mouw, Marianne Meye Thompson, James Bradley, and James Butler for the deposit they made in my life during that week in Pasadena.

Chapter Comments

13. Emil's interpretation of Angie's dream came out of a conversation I had with my friend about her real dream. Again, she has graciously given permission for me to use it.

14. My first encounter with the word *prevenience* came from Eugene Peterson's book, *The Contemplative Pastor: Returning to the Art of Spiritual Direction* (Grand Rapids, MI: William B. Eerdmans Publishing Company, 1993).

    The quote from John Wesley is taken from his letter to Miss March, June 9, 1774 (Accessed 7/4/05, http://wesley.nnu.edu/john_wesley/letters/1775.htm. Wesley Center Online, Northwest Nazarene University).

15. I find the image of the crashing elevator an apt metaphor for the way too many people I know view the destinies of their lives.

16. I struggled with the decision to include abortion as an issue for Angie. I didn't want the story to be about the ethics related to abortion. I decided to keep it in because it helped Angie to wrestle with the idea of God's love.

17. I'm thankful to my friend Marianne, who walked me through the *Me, Why?*, and *God* exercise as she helped me to come to grips with my own fears and self-judgments.

18. After two years of learning and building relationships with my doctoral cohort at George Fox Evangelical Seminary through emails, chat rooms, and discussion boards, I thought it would be good for Paul and his friends to move part of their discussion into cyberspace.

19. The book that really helped me to think in new ways about the significance of the death of Jesus was *Recovering the Scandal of the Cross: Atonement in New Testament & Contemporary Contexts* by Joel Green and Mark Baker (Downers Grove, IL: InterVarsity Press, 2000).

20. My apologies to my friend Rick, whose last name I borrowed for Gracie. Gracie started out to be a solid partner with Paul and Dean, even coming up with solutions to the problem of redirecting the church. Unfortunately, she morphed into the role of the prime antagonist. I just couldn't stop her.

The Bartender

21. Paul's dismissive observation of Angie made me think of the sadness that often lies behind the life-worn eyes of the people in my world. The good news is for them.

22. The pain and turmoil with which families of pastors have to live is too familiar for people in vocational ministry. Contrary to popular belief, these folks do not have an unending capacity for grief.

23. This scene was inspired by an experience I had many years ago as a Christian school principal. A man in the sponsoring church asked to address the board on an issue about which he was upset, only to send in his place another man who worked for an extreme, right-wing anti-communist group. The meeting did not go well.

24. F. M. Lehman was my great-grandfather. He died when I was a baby, but I knew my great-grandmother well. This song is one of his hits. (*Songs That Are Different*. Kansas City, MO: Nazarene Publishing House, 1917, 1945)

25. Paul's thoughts about "... going with God's Spirit into the world" was inspired by Karl Barth's statement in *Church Dogmatics*:

    > Solidarity with the world means that those who are genuinely pious approach the children of the world as such, that those who are genuinely righteous are not ashamed to sit down with the unrighteous as friends, that those who are genuinely wise do not hesitate to seem to be fools among fools, and that those who are genuinely holy are not too good or irreproachable to go down into 'hell' in a very secular fashion ... Since Jesus Christ is the Savior of the world, [the church] can exist in worldly fashion, not unwillingly nor with a bad conscience, but willingly and with a good conscience. It consists in the recognition that its members also bear in themselves and in some way actualize all human possibilities. (CD, IV/3, pp. 773–4)

26. The chapters 26–28 are facilitated by the crisis of an impending abortion, but, again, the ethics of abortion are not the point here. The crisis of Angie's decision is drawing Emil into his own crisis of faith and mission.

27. I've never been inside an abortion clinic but I have to believe they have security systems.

Chapter Comments

28. I wrote this chapter the day after seeing the movie, *The Chronicles of Narnia*. This scene made me think of the way Narnia called the children back into it, not only for the purpose of serving Aslan, but also because it was their true home.

29. Thanks to my friend Merrilee, who explained to me how quickly an early-term abortion procedure can be completed and the ability of the patient to leave unassisted.

30. As much as email can be a benefit, it also affords people the opportunity to terminate relationships at the click of a button.

31. Father Tom, while not a main character, seemed to offer the presence of an ancient-future faith. He represents an ancient tradition but also incarnates the love of Jesus as he encounters the broken and rejected of the world.

E. The quotation by Vincent Van Gogh is from *The Encyclopedia of Religious Quotations* (Westwood, New Jersey: Fleming H. Revell Company, 1965), 279.

The story about the woman's encounter in the park is based on a similar event that happened to a South African woman who attended my church. These things really happen.

www.ingramcontent.com/pod-product-compliance
Lightning Source LLC
Chambersburg PA
CBHW070919160426
43193CB00011B/1523